My Catholic Morals!

My Catholic Morals!

Volume Three of Three

My Catholic Life! Series

By

John Paul Thomas

My Catholic Life!
www.myCatholic.Life

ISBN-13: 978-0692528198
ISBN-10: 0692528199

DEDICATION

To our Blessed Mother. Her maternal care for us, her perfect surrender to the will of God and her powerful intercession are gifts beyond measure. May her heart shine through these pages and may her own life of perfect beatitude inspire us to live holy lives.

BY

JOHN PAUL THOMAS

"John Paul Thomas" is a pen name this author picked in honor of the Apostles Saints John and Thomas and the great evangelist Saint Paul. This name also evokes the memory of the great Pope Saint John Paul II.

John is the beloved Apostle who sought out a deeply personal and intimate relationship with his Savior. Hopefully the writings in this book point us all to a deeply personal and intimate relationship with our God. May John be a model of this intimacy and love.

Thomas is also a beloved Apostle and close friend of Jesus but is well known for his lack of faith in Jesus' resurrection. Though he ultimately entered into a profound faith crying out, "my Lord and my God," he is given to us as a model of our own weakness of faith. Thomas should inspire us to always return to faith when we realize we have doubted.

As a Pharisee, Paul severely persecuted the early Christian Church. However, after going through a powerful conversion, he went on to become the great evangelist to the gentiles, founding many new communities of believers and writing many letters contained in Sacred Scripture. His letters are deeply personal and reveal a shepherd's heart. He is a model for all as we seek to embrace our calling to spread the Gospel.

My Catholic Life! Series

An introduction to this three volume series

The *My Catholic Life! Series* is a three volume series written as a complete summary of our glorious Catholic faith! The goal of these books is to answer the difficult and deep questions of life in a clear and understandable way. We need to know who we are and what life is all about. We need to know who God is and what He has spoken to us through the ages.

Volume One, *My Catholic Faith!* is a summary of the Apostles' and Nicene Creeds. This volume looks at everything from the creation of the world to God's eternal plan of salvation. Other topics include: The afterlife, the Trinity, saints, our Blessed Mother, faith, and the Church. It is a summary of the teaching of the *Catechism of the Catholic Church* #1-1065.

Volume Two, *My Catholic Worship!* is a summary of the life of grace found in prayer and the Sacraments. So often the Sacraments can be seen as dry and empty rituals. But they are, in reality, the greatest treasures we have! They are God's true presence among us! This book is a summary of the *Catechism of the Catholic Church* #1066-1690 and #2558-2865.

Volume Three, *My Catholic Morals!* is a summary of Catholic moral teaching. It reveals the moral principles of our faith as well as a summary of all our Church's moral teachings. It is a summary of the *Catechism of the Catholic Church* #1691-2557.

Table of Contents

Introduction

We are all called to be saints! This is what we are made for and this is the only way to happiness. Life in Christ, a life lived according to the will of God, is the only way to live out our dignity and to experience the freedom we so long for. This book helps to shed light on the glorious calling we have received to become saints. A life of sin leads to death and despair, a life of grace and moral uprightness leads to happiness. This is a simple truth that we must all discover and live.

In the first volume of this series, we looked at what we believe, especially as presented in the Creed we profess at Mass every Sunday. The second volume of this series presented our life of prayer and worship, especially in the Sacraments. The Sacraments were seen as real and personal ways of encountering the Living God and letting Him enter in and transform our lives. This volume completes our reflections on our Catholic life by revealing how we are called to live. It reveals the effect of coming to believe all that is contained in our Creed with a deep faith and surrendering to God through a life of prayer, worship and the Sacraments. The effect of faith and worship is a life lived in Christ. And a life lived in Christ is our life of morality.

Catholic morality is often seen in a negative way. We often think morality is about "what I can't do." It's true that Christ's teachings on the moral life limit us from engaging in actions contrary to His will and contrary to our dignity. But morality is so much more than just a list of restrictions. Morality is also about living in freedom! It's about living in the freedom that our Triune God has in store for us. Conversely, sin is a slavery. And when we give in to sin, especially serious and habitual sin, we lose our dignity and the freedom in which God wants us to live our lives.

Morality is also about embracing a life of virtue. It's all about what I'm called to do in a positive way. And the "positive way" we are called to live is through a life of virtue. Virtues are spiritual habits that strengthen us to live good and morally upright lives. Just as sin can become a bad habit, so also virtue can become a good habit. Therefore, this book will delve into some of the most important virtues we can embrace.

Lastly, morality is about living even beyond virtue. It's a calling to live in beatitude. "Beatitude" is a supernatural way of living that only makes sense in Christ. We need His wisdom and His grace to live holy lives embracing the Beatitudes He taught.

This book will be broken up into two main parts. The first part will focus upon what we call the moral principles. Learning about these moral principles will provide us with a sort of foundation to understand the particulars of a life lived in Christ. We'll learn about moral decision making, the moral law of God, grace, the conscience, sin, mercy, our connection to others and much more.

The second part of this book will carefully go through each of the Ten Commandments and present specific moral laws of God. Some of these will be seen as "thou shall not..." But we will also look at each of the commandments in the positive. This means that each commandment will also be looked at in light of the ways we are called to happiness and fulfillment through the moral law of God.

Hopefully, this book will give you a greater understanding of the way God calls us to live as well as an understanding of why He does. May the Holy Spirit be with you as you dive into *My Catholic Morality!*

1

WHO AM I?

I Am an *Imago Dei*

Do you know who you are? That may seem like an odd question but it's worth pondering. Who are you? Who are you in your deepest core? What is it that makes you who you are?

Often times we take our identity in all sorts of meaningless things. We take our identity in what we have accomplished, in how we look, in who our friends are, in how we are perceived by others. But, truth be told, none of that matters. It really doesn't. What matters is what God thinks and who He sees when He looks at you.

When God looks at you He sees two things. First, yes, He sees your sins, all of them. He is fully aware of every weakness and every dysfunction in your life. Nothing is hidden from the eyes of God!

But fear not. He also sees something else. He sees who you are at your core and who He wants you to be. He looks at you and sees an image of Himself. He sees a reflection of His own beauty and splendor. He sees an *imago Dei*, an image of God.

We must also see, within our soul, an image of God. We must see that God loves us so much that He sent His Son, Jesus, to come and dwell with us. And He not only dwells *with* us, He also dwells *within* us.

When we can come to discover Christ living within us, we will begin to discover our true dignity and, in that discovery, begin to live as we ought.

The moral life is all about discovering who we are, a discovery of Christ living within us. When we allow Christ to live within us, we begin to live the life He wants us to live. We begin to live a morally upright and holy life. And in this living, we become who we are. Jesus reveals who we are and we embrace that life more fully.

The Beatitudes

Blessed are the poor in spirit, for theirs is the kingdom of heaven.
Blessed are they who mourn, for they will be comforted.
Blessed are the meek, for they will inherit the land.
Blessed are they who hunger and thirst for righteousness, for they will be satisfied.
Blessed are the merciful, for they will be shown mercy.
Blessed are the clean of heart, for they will see God.
Blessed are the peacemakers, for they will be called children of God.
Blessed are they who are persecuted for the sake of righteousness, for theirs is the kingdom of heaven.
Blessed are you when they insult you and persecute you and utter every kind of evil against you [falsely] because of me. Rejoice and be glad, for your reward will be great in heaven. Thus they persecuted the prophets who were before you. (Mt 5:3-12)

If we want to discover who we are and who we are called to become we must understand the Beatitudes. The Beatitudes are the pinnacle of the Christian moral life. To live the Beatitudes is to live in Christ. But that is easier said than done.

The Beatitudes present us with a challenge of love followed with a glorious reward for our faithful living of that challenge. To be poor in spirit, mourn (over sin), to be meek, to long for righteousness, etc., is a high calling. And to accept persecution joyfully is not an easy thing to do. But the end result is that we obtain Heaven, are children of God, are satisfied and see God! The struggle is worth the blessing.

A beatitude is a blessing. It's the blessing of living fully in God's grace rather than just living by our own ideas. It's seeking a higher calling and embracing it in faith rather than full sight. In other words, embracing the Beatitudes requires that God speaks to us in our hearts, reveals His mysterious and profound will to us found in the wisdom of the Beatitudes, and gives us the grace we need to live them. This takes a lot of surrender to God and a lot of trust in His wisdom. But when a person can believe the wisdom of the Beatitudes and live in accord with their high calling, there is an outpouring of grace and joy that fills that person. There is a tremendous "blessing" that fills the one who lives in accord with this grace.

We discussed in Book One of this series the desire we all have for happiness. The Beatitudes are the ultimate fulfillment of this desire. By living the Beatitudes one discovers that God and God alone satisfies, and that living in communion with Him is well worth any hardship or struggle we must endure in life. But believing this takes a great grace! It takes the gift of faith and knowledge. It takes a special action of God in our lives.

Much could be said about the Beatitudes, but for now just try to spend some time pondering them and trying to understand that they are the pinnacle of the Christian moral life. Put that truth in the back of your mind and try not to forget it.

The Effects of Freedom

Living a life in the Beatitudes requires that we live a life of true freedom. Additionally, living the Beatitudes brings that freedom. It's a sort of cyclical action in our lives. True freedom opens us to the Beatitudes and the Beatitudes fill us with greater freedom to discover them and live them.

What does it mean to be free? Too often we associate "freedom" with "free will." We think that we are free when we do *what* we want, *when* we want, *because* we want. Our culture has a strong focus on human liberty and human rights. But it's so very easy to arrive at a false sense of what freedom truly is.

So what is freedom? It's not the ability to do *what we want*; rather, it's the ability to do *what we ought*. Freedom is found in the conscious choice to do the will of God and, in embracing that will, to live in accord with our dignity.

It's true that God gave us free will. We have a mind and a will and are endowed with an ability to make our own moral choices. This is a sacred gift that goes to the heart of who we are. But it's only in the proper exercise of this free will that we obtain authentic human freedom. And the opposite is also true. In exercising our free will in the negative, in the free choice to embrace sin, we become slaves of that sin and our dignity is greatly compromised.

When we are faced with making a moral decision, there are many factors to consider so as to determine the morality of our choice and the effects that these choices will have on us. For example, the *Catechism* identifies five factors that could affect us: Ignorance, duress, fear, and other psychological or social factors. Each one of these factors has the potential to confuse us in making the right decision. As a result of that confusion, we are hindered in our ability to act properly. What this tells us is that, if we want to be truly free and if we want to make good choices in life, we must strive to be free of the pressures and temptations that these factors impose upon us. In other words, we must strive to be fully aware of the moral decisions before us, be free of fear and duress, and understand and overcome any psychological or social influences that could cloud our decision making.

Take, for example, a crime of passion. There are numerous ways this could be played out. Generally speaking, try to imagine a situation when someone acts out immorally because of some extreme influence upon them beyond their control. Perhaps they are filled with such fear that they react out of that fear and act contrary to the moral law in anger or fright. Or take, for example, the person who has never had the benefit of having the will of God clearly explained to them. Instead, their whole life they have been raised in an environment that "preached" some contrary moral value. They were truly ignorant of the moral truth and, therefore, are ignorant of the fact that some of their actions are contrary to the moral law.

In both of these situations, a person may act in a way contrary to the will of God. But, at the same time, because of factors out of their control, they may not be fully responsible for their poor choice. God is the only one who knows all the details and He will sort it out.

More will be said on this in the coming chapters but, for now, it's important to understand this so that we can understand the value of moral decision making. By understanding the fact that we are sometimes not fully responsible for the poor decisions we make, we should also come to the conclusion that, when we are fully aware of the moral factors involved in a decision, and then make the right and good decision, there are glorious consequences for the good. Through those good choices we experience the true freedom we are called to have and we grow in the dignity we have been given as God's beloved children.

Making Moral Choices

So what is a moral choice? Perhaps that sounds like an overly philosophical question. It may be but it's an important question that has very real and very practical implications. By understanding the basic makeup of a moral decision, we will be in a much better position to make the right choices in life.

The *Catechism* presents us with the three basic sources of morality and moral decision making. We'll look at these three sources carefully because it's important to understand.

The morality of human acts depends on:

—the object chosen;
—the end in view or the intention;
—the circumstances of the action.

The object, the intention, and the circumstances make up the "sources," or constitutive elements, of the morality of human acts. (#1750)

Don't get lost in this language. Let's look at each part of a moral act so that you can more clearly understand your own actions and the morality involved. This will especially be helpful later in the book as we consider specific moral questions.

Object Chosen: The "object chosen" specifically refers to the action we choose to do. Some actions are always wrong. We call these "intrinsically evil" actions. For example, murder (the taking of an innocent life) is always wrong. Other examples of intrinsically evil actions would be things like blasphemy and adultery. There is never any justification for an intrinsically evil action.

Some actions could be considered morally good all the time by their very nature. For example, an act of mercy or forgiveness is always good.

All other actions are morally neutral in and of themselves. For example, throwing a ball is morally neutral unless the <u>circumstances</u> (as we'll see below) are such that you're throwing the ball at the neighbor's window with the <u>intention</u> of breaking the window. But the act all by itself, the act of throwing a ball, is neither good nor bad. That's why we need to also consider the intention and circumstance of a neutral action.

The most important things to consider with actions, then, are that some acts in and of themselves are always intrinsically evil and should never be done. Some are always good: acts of faith, hope and charity. And some are morally neutral by themselves.

The Intention: The intention of an action plays a significant role in determining whether or not the action is morally good or bad. The intention can have the effect of undermining what appears to be a good action and making it evil. For example, if someone gives money to a children's home as a donation, this seems like a good action. But if that donation is done because the person is a politician and it's nothing more than a selfish show to gain public support and praise, then the apparently good act suddenly becomes disordered and sinful.

Furthermore, an intrinsically evil action can never become good based on a good intention. For example, a direct lie is a disordered action. One never accomplishes a good act by lying, even if it's done with an apparently good intention. "The end does not justify the means."

Circumstances: The circumstances surrounding a good or evil act are important. The circumstances cannot make an act good or evil, but they can affect the moral responsibility one has. For example, if someone lies, this is a wrong action. However, if they are under extreme fear and lie within this context, they most likely are not nearly as morally responsible for the lie as someone who deliberately lies in normal circumstance. Extreme fear or other similar circumstances do not make lying good or even neutral; rather, it only affects how responsible one is for the action.

The circumstances also can contribute to the moral goodness of an action. For example, take telling the truth. Say that same person is under extreme emotional fear and, despite the temptation to fear, is truthful anyway in a virtuous and courageous way. That act of courage becomes morally magnified for the good as a result of the difficult circumstance.

Hopefully this brief reflection upon the three sources of morality help give insight into moral decision making. If it seems a bit confusing still, do not worry. For now, just try to grasp the basic principles. It should become much clearer as we go through specific and concrete examples later in this book.

Good vs. good

It may be helpful here to offer a distinction between what we may call "Good" and "good." That may seem like a strange distinction at first so let me explain.

First, we can define Good (with a capital "G") as anything and everything that makes up part of God's plan for our lives. Good, in this sense, is also what is truly beneficial for us in the mind and will of God.

Second, we can speak in a more philosophical language of "good" (with a small "g"). In this sense, we are referring to anything that our mind, will, desires, feelings or passions are drawn to. Sometimes, these goods are not part of God's plan and, therefore, are not truly Good.

Sound confusing? Not really, it's just a philosophical distinction that we need in order to understand ourselves and God's plan for our lives.

Let me offer an example of a "good" that is not "Good" for us. Take the person who deeply desires to get drunk. Why do they desire and choose this? Because they erroneously see it as something that is good for them in the moment. We all know it's not truly Good and is not part of God's plan for them, but, in this case, they choose it anyway because their passion, desires or emotions overwhelm their mind and lead them to choose that which is unhealthy.

Another less clear example may be exercise. Say a person regularly exercises but, over time, becomes obsessed with it. They start to use what normally could be Good in an excessive way. In this case, exercise is a good, but not <u>G</u>ood. Got it? If not, don't worry just yet. Read on and it will hopefully make more sense.

Passions, Feelings and Emotions

In creating us, God gave us passions, feelings and emotions. These parts of our soul are normal and are good in so far as they are part of who we are. But these appetites can lead to evil or to good based on what they become attached to.

The normal way these spiritual appetites work is that they are drawn to the good and repulsed by evil. However, they are also easily deceived. It is very possible for a passion to be drawn to what it perceives as good, but in fact is actually evil. For example, say someone longs to be rich. In their mind they have deceptively come to believe that wealth is the answer to their problems. They then come across an opportunity to make a quick fortune, but it involves deception and malice. It's entirely possible that their passion will push them to act in this deceptive way anyway because they have allowed themselves to become convinced of the great value of money.

Or perhaps a clearer example is the passion of love. Very often the reason a married person has an affair is because he/she has allowed the natural passion of love to overwhelm his/her human reason and choose the affair even though it's sinful.

Passions are powerful forces. But passions are ultimately able to be used for good when we make God and His will the good we seek. In this case, the person "falls in love" with God and His holy will. They then "passionately" choose what God has revealed because they desire to please God and express their love for Him.

Feelings and emotions are closely related to passions and follow the same basic principles. The key in understanding these parts of who we are is to understand that whatever we choose in our minds as a good, our passions, desires, feelings and emotions will ultimately follow. They may not follow right away, but in time they will. And the perfection of the human person is achieved when one's entire being (mind, soul, heart and strength) is caught up in the true good, namely, in God.

Conscience

The conscience is a glorious gift of God! It's the secret core within us, a sacred sanctuary where we meet God. One of the most quoted passages from the Vatican II Council comes from a document called *Gaudium et Spes*, and offers a very beautiful description of the conscience:

> Deep within his conscience man discovers a law which he has not laid upon himself but which he must obey. Its voice, ever calling him to love and to do what is good and to avoid evil, sounds in his heart at the right moment.... For man has in his heart a law inscribed by God.... His conscience is man's most secret core and his sanctuary. There he is alone with God whose voice echoes in his depths. (GS 16)

Our conscience is that place within where we make moral decisions. It's a place that can become deeply confused and distorted, but it's ideally a place of great peace, clarity and joy. It's ideally the place where we analyze our moral decisions, clearly understand them, allow God and our human reason to prevail, and then freely choose that which is good and right. When one does this there is the reward of great peace and an affirmation of one's dignity. Within the conscience one takes responsibility for both good and evil actions.

The conscience is the place within where the law of God comes in contact with our practical circumstances in life. It's the place within where we are able to analyze the actions we are considering as well as the actions we have done in light of the moral law of God.

Regarding actions we are considering, the conscience is the place where the truth hopefully prevails and directs our actions for the good. Regarding actions of the past, when we analyze these actions and judge them to be sinful, the conscience is the place where we are challenged to repent and seek God's mercy and forgiveness. It's not so much a place where we are filled with guilt and remorse; rather, it's a place where we see our sin and offer it to the mercy of God with hope of forgiveness and healing.

By analogy, as we read in the passage above from Vatican II, the conscience is a sanctuary within. Therefore, we should see it as something similar to the sanctuary within a church. In the old days there was an altar railing marking off the sanctuary indicating, in part, that the sanctuary was a sacred place where the presence of God resided in a unique way. It is the place of reservation of the Blessed Sacrament and the place of the sacred altar. So, also, we should see our conscience as a sacred sanctuary within. There, in that sanctuary, we meet God. We hear Him, love Him and freely obey Him. It is our deepest core and the place of interior worship.

The conscience must be respected. For example, think about the Sacrament of Confession. In that Sacrament the person invites the priest into the sanctuary of their conscience. They invite the priest to see their sin and, in the Person of Christ, to absolve it. The Church imposes upon the priest the requirement of the sacred "seal of Confession." This "seal" means he is forbidden, under any circumstances, to reveal what was revealed to him. What does this mean? One of the things it means is that the conscience, into which he is invited through Confession, is so personal, private and sacred, that no one has a right to be there except for Christ and those whom the individual freely invites in.

No one has a right to see another's conscience through force or manipulation. Instead, we as Christians must recognize the sacredness of that inner sanctuary of each person and treat it with the utmost respect.

The sacredness of conscience must also be respected as a person grows in faith. Growth in faith and conversion must be handled with the greatest of care. For example, when Christians are preaching the Gospel, it's essential that we make sure we are respecting others' consciences. One danger that must be avoided is what we call "proselytism." Proselytism is a sort of pressuring or manipulation of another to convert. It may be done through fear, harshness, intimidation, and the like. For that reason, the preacher of the Gospel must be careful that "conversion" does not happen through some form of force. A classic example would be the extreme "fire and brimstone" homily that causes the weak-minded person to "convert" out of fear of Hell. Sure, we should be afraid of Hell, but grace and salvation must be offered to people, in their conscience, as an invitation of love first and foremost. Only in this way is a conversion truly a conversion of the heart.

As Christians and as humans, we have a moral duty to form our conscience in accord with what is true. The formation of our conscience takes place by being open to all that is present to our human reason and all that God reveals to us in the depths of our hearts. This is not as hard as it may at first sound. If you reflect upon this you'll find it makes perfect sense and is deeply rational, so read on.

First, human reason can come to discern what is true and what is false on the most basic of levels. *The natural law* is a law that God wrote upon our conscience and is there ready for us to understand and embrace. We know, for example, that stealing, lying, murder and the like are wrong. How do we know? We just know as a result of these moral laws being inscribed upon our conscience. But how do you know, you ask? You just know! God made you that way. The natural moral law is there within us and acknowledging it is like a light bulb going off within. It makes sense.

In addition to the natural law that all humans have access to in their conscience, there is also the divine law of revelation. This *revelation* of the divine law refers to the will of God that can only be known by hearing His voice within. It often comes to us by the reading of Scripture, the teachings of the Church, or the wisdom of the saints. But ultimately, when one of these external sources of God's Word is presented to us, we must then internalize it by allowing that Word to also speak to our heart. Again, this experience may be like a "light bulb moment" similar to the discovery of the natural law within. Only this time the "light bulb" requires a special gift of faith to understand.

The problem is that, all too often, we can allow various influences to confuse us and mislead our conscience. The most common causes of a confused conscience are disordered passions, fear, irrational arguments, habitual sin and ignorance of the truth. Sometimes we can even be confused by a false understanding of love. The *Catechism* identifies the following as common sources of an erroneous conscience:

> Ignorance of Christ and his Gospel, bad example given by others, enslavement to one's passions, assertion of a mistaken notion of autonomy of conscience, rejection of the Church's authority and her teaching, lack of conversion and of charity: these can be at the source of errors of judgment in moral conduct. (#1792)

Nonetheless, when a person strives to have a well-formed conscience, he/she is obliged to follow that conscience and act accordingly.

With that said, it's also important to point out two types of erroneous judgments. One is an erroneous conscience that is culpable (sinful) and the other is one which is not culpable (not personally sinful even though it's still misinformed).

Erroneous Conscience: Am I Guilty?

Sometimes, as explained above, people make wrong choices and believe they are making right choices. So are they guilty of sin if they make a wrong choice believing it is the right choice? For example, we know that abortion is intrinsically evil, meaning, it is always wrong to take the innocent life of a child within the womb. But what about a person who honestly believes that abortion is OK to do in some circumstances? Let's say they get pregnant out of wedlock and pregnancy at the time will interfere with a college education. Is it OK, sometimes, to have an abortion?

The answer is clearly "no." It is never good to have an abortion and the action, in and of itself, is always wrong. It's important to look at the wrong action of abortion by itself, but it's also important to consider the moral guilt or personal sinfulness (or not) of those committing this act. Read this carefully so that it's not misunderstood. We can easily fall into what we call "moral relativism" if we are not careful. Moral relativism is a way of saying, for example, that abortion may be wrong for me but it may not be wrong for you. That's a misunderstanding. However, it may be truthful to say that some people are more morally guilty of that sin whereas others, out of honest ignorance, may do a wrong action without being personally sinful. Again, try to carefully understand this. Here is an example:

First, consider a young woman who was raised in a household that practiced no faith whatsoever. Through no fault of her own, she never heard people say that abortion was wrong. Let's say that both her parents were physicians who regularly performed abortions and they spoke freely about their conviction that they were doing good and helping women. This young girl hears this throughout her life and is never exposed to the contrary argument. Again, *through no fault of her own* she never learns that abortion is wrong.

In this context, let's say she gets pregnant out of wedlock just before going off to college. Her parents find out and they smile and tell her all will be well and they will bring her to the clinic on Monday to help her with this problem. She agrees and has the abortion thinking she is doing the right thing.

Now, it's important to point out clearly here that only God knows her heart and only God knows if she went forward with an abortion truly believing it was good. It must be said that, objectively speaking, she made an erroneous decision. The act of abortion is intrinsically evil and is wrong in every way. But the question here is whether or not she personally sinned in her choice or if she made the wrong choice *through no fault of her own*. It's hard to believe, today, in our day and age, that someone would never be exposed to the truth about the evil of abortion. But, nonetheless, in this example, let's just say, for the sake of argument, that she really did not know it was wrong and that she truly didn't ever have an opportunity to be exposed to the truth of this situation. Furthermore, let's say, for the sake of this example, that she sincerely believed abortion in this case was good and right. Given these circumstances did she personally sin? She may not have. Did she do a wrong action? Yes she did. Abortion is the wrong action but she may not be held accountable for it before God in this case.

What this shows us is that it is possible to do the wrong action and not have personal responsibility for that action. Again, this only applies to the case where someone has a misinformed and, therefore, erroneous conscience *through no fault of their own*.

With that said, if there was negligence on her part in seeking the truth. Or if she had been presented with the truth and refused to be open. Or if there were any other factors that led to her erroneous decision which were her fault, then she would bear some responsibility. Perhaps her guilt would be minimal, or perhaps her guilt would be great. Only God knows the heart. But our purpose here is to try to understand the difference between a wrongful action and personal guilt for that action.

One important point to add to this explanation is that all of us do have a personal duty to seek the truth and to properly inform our conscience.

We must take responsibility for a misinformed conscience when we are negligent. But, nonetheless, God knows our particular circumstances and will judge accordingly.

Growth in Virtue and the Gifts of the Holy Spirit

There are four wonderful gifts God gave us to live a good moral life and to achieve holiness. These gifts will help us within our consciences to make good decisions in life and to understand right from wrong. These gifts are as follows: 1) the four human virtues; 2) the three theological virtues; 3) the seven gifts of the Spirit; and 4) the twelve fruits of the Holy Spirit.

Four Human Virtues:

We begin with the four human virtues: prudence, justice, fortitude and temperance. These four virtues, being "human" virtues, "are stable dispositions of the intellect and the will that govern our acts, order our passions, and guide our conduct in accordance with reason and faith" (*CCC* #1834). The key distinction between the four "human virtues" and the three "theological virtues" is that human virtues are acquired by our own human effort. We work toward them and have the power in our own intellect and will to form these virtues within. In contrast, the theological virtues are acquired only by a gift of grace from God and are, therefore, infused by God. Let's take a look at each one of these human virtues.

Prudence: The virtue of prudence is the gift we use to take the more general moral principles given us by God and apply them to concrete and real life situations. It's the ability to use the moral law in our daily life. It connects the law to our particular situation in life. Prudence is also considered the "Mother of all Virtue" in that it directs all the rest. It is a sort of foundational virtue that enables us to make good moral judgments and decisions. Prudence strengthens us to act in accord with God's will. Prudence is primarily an exercise of our intellect in that it enables us to make good practical judgments within our conscience.

Justice: Our relationship with God as well as our relationship with others requires we offer them the proper love and respect they deserve. Justice, like prudence, enables us to concretely apply the moral principles of proper respect of God and others to concrete situations. Justice toward God takes on an attitude of proper reverence and worship in that we are able to know how God wants us to revere Him and worship Him here and now. Similarly, justice toward others enables us to treat them in accord with their rights and dignity. We just know what love and respect look like in our daily interactions with them.

Fortitude: This virtue produces strength to ensure "firmness in difficulties and constancy in the pursuit of the good" (*CCC* #1808). This virtue helps in two ways. First, it helps us to choose what is good even if it requires great strength. Choosing the good is not always easy. At times, it requires great sacrifice and even suffering. Fortitude provides the strength we need to choose the good even when difficult. Second, it also enables one to avoid that which is evil. Just as it can be hard to choose the good, so also it can be hard to avoid evil and temptation. Temptations, at times, can be strong and overwhelming. A person with fortitude is able to face that temptation toward evil and avoid it.

Temperance: There are many things in this world that are desirous and enticing. Some of these things are not part of God's will for us. Temperance "moderates the attraction of pleasures and provides balance in the use of created goods" (*CCC* #1809). In other words, it helps with self-control and keeps all our desires and emotions in check. The desires, passions and emotions can be very powerful forces. They draw us in many directions. Ideally, they draw us to embrace the will of God and all that is good. But when they are attached to that which is not God's will, temperance moderates these human aspects of our body and soul keeping them in check and in control so that they do not control us.

As mentioned above, these four virtues are acquired by human effort and discipline. However, they can also be drawn up into God's grace and take on a supernatural character. They can be elevated to a new level and strengthen us beyond what we could ever achieve by our own human effort. This is done by prayer and surrender to God.

Three Theological Virtues:

The four human virtues are not enough to live a full and holy Christian life. We need more. We need supernatural gifts from God called the theological virtues. These virtues are faith, hope and charity. They are "supernatural" in that we cannot obtain them by ourselves. They are infused into our souls directly from God when we are open to them and they animate and transform the human virtues mentioned above to that new supernatural level. They enable the Christian to live in accord with the mind and will of God in all things. They especially enable us to live the Christian life to a degree that is beyond our own human potential. This is key since there is no way we can live a holy Christian life by our own effort.

Faith: This virtue is "the theological virtue by which we believe in God and believe all that he has said and revealed to us, and that Holy Church proposes for our belief" (*CCC* #1814). Faith is a very easy virtue to misunderstand. It can be thought that faith is just believing that which we cannot know. Or perhaps even a sort of wishful thinking. But faith is so much more. Faith is KNOWING God and all that God reveals. It's a sort of sixth sense we have on a spiritual level which enables us to know beyond our natural human capacity. God infuses a certain knowledge of Himself and His will and we ascent to believe it. When this happens, it produces a true certainty within us. In other words, it produces a firm conviction for the truth which we could never arrive at by ourselves. In fact, it ultimately produces a conviction and knowledge so deep that we can come to believe on a level that is beyond any human knowing. For example, no one would disagree that 2+2=4. We know this by our human reason. Faith is a knowledge that goes deeper and provides a conviction that is stronger even than the human knowledge of mathematics or that which we know by our sight, smell, touch, hearing and smelling. With faith we know because God reveals truth to us and He is the one guaranteeing this truth. Therefore, the conviction and certainty is the deepest form of knowledge we can have.

Hope: As reflected upon in the first book, we all desire happiness. It's in our nature. We cannot shake this desire. Hope is the theological virtue that enables us to fulfill this desire in accord with God's will. It helps keep our eyes on the Kingdom of Heaven and all that God wills for us. It points us to eternal beatitude and helps our desires to move past the temporary things of this world to the eternal aspects of God's Kingdom. It enables us to rely upon the power and strength of the Holy Spirit to stay in God's grace and live by the faith we have been given. In other words, hope is a supernatural gift that enables us to see the potential fulfillment of our lives by seeing the goal of Christian living. We see God's will, we see the blessings attached to His will, and we know we can obtain them by His help. This supernatural knowledge gives us strength and energy to pursue that which we could never pursue by our own human ability.

Charity: Without Charity, we have nothing (1 Corinthians 13). Charity is the grace we need to love God with our whole heart, mind, soul and strength and to love our neighbor. Charity is manifest in our lives when both faith and hope are alive and active. Faith is primarily an act of the intellect, hope is especially an act of the will, and that combination produces the pure and holy love we call charity. Charity is the fulfillment of all laws of God. It's a supernatural gift by which we are able to overcome all things that keep us from perfection and holiness. In fact, charity and holiness are synonymous. If a person is filled with charity, that person is holy. When charity is perfected, the soul is perfected. This is the greatest of all virtues!

Charity is not just doing kind actions. It is first and foremost an act toward God. The perfection of Charity toward God means our whole being is consumed with love of God. We are set aflame with love of Him and are given a powerful drive to seek Him and love Him above all things. We discover His will in charity and are able to fulfill it because we want to fulfill it.

As we fall deeply in love with God and His divine will, we will also be consumed with a love of others. We will be directed, by the Holy Spirit, toward those whom God wants us to offer a special gift of His grace, love and mercy. We will desire to show mercy and we will find great satisfaction in offering to others all that God wants us to offer. Charity will sustain and fill us beyond anything else in life.

Gifts of the Holy Spirit: The Gifts of the Holy Spirit are gifts from God that we are all called to obtain in their fullness. They help us on our path toward Christian holiness. In fact, they are *essential* gifts we must strive for in our lives. Each one of these gifts must reside in the Christian soul that desires perfection. They are permanent dispositions within us that enable us to follow the promptings and guidance of the Holy Spirit in our lives. They are seven ways that we are open to and receive the Holy Spirit. The seven Gifts of the Holy Spirit are:

Wisdom
Understanding
Counsel
Fortitude
Knowledge
Piety
Fear of the Lord

For a more detailed explanation of each gift see Book Two of this series in the chapter on Confirmation.

Fruits of the Spirit: Just as an apple tree produces apples, so the Holy Spirit alive in our hearts produces spiritual fruit. These fruits are traditionally numbered as twelve and are: charity, joy, peace, patience, kindness, goodness, generosity, gentleness, faithfulness, modesty, self-control, chastity. These fruits are the blessings of living a good moral life in Christ!

Sin: The Good, the Bad and the Ugly

Perhaps your first question, after reading the title of this section, is, "What could be good about sin?" Sure, we realize it is "bad" and even "ugly," but how can it be "good?"

The answer is simple. God's almighty power is just that: ALMIGHTY! And, as a result, He can take even our sin and transform it. This doesn't mean that sin itself is good; rather, it means that God can transform sin in our lives. He can bring goodness out of anything and the primary way He does this is by His mercy.

St. Paul said, in his letter to the Romans, "where sin increased, grace overflowed all the more" (Romans 5:20). God saw our fallenness, He sees our sin and His response is first and foremost to offer mercy and grace. He desires to forgive us and reconcile with us. And it is this grace, given as a result of our sin, that is "good" beyond what we can ever comprehend.

With this foundational understanding of the good God can bring out of sin, let's now look at the "bad" and the "ugly" parts.

> Sin is an offense against reason, truth, and right conscience; it is failure in genuine love for God and neighbor caused by a perverse attachment to certain goods. (*CCC* #1849)

Sin, as an "offense," is an action we perform, or an omission of what we ought to do. It's an action that is opposed to "reason, truth and right conscience." This is a helpful insight because it shows us that when someone commits a sin, they are acting foolishly and in a way that is in opposition to reality. They must deny the truth within their conscience in order to complete any sinful act willfully.

Sin is also the result of "a perverse attachment to certain goods." This means that sin comes as a result of becoming attached to a "good" in a disordered way. This may, at first, seem like a strange thing to say. How can it be wrong to be attached to something that is "good?"

To understand this properly we have to understand what a "good" is. A good, in this sense, is anything that our mind and will perceive as good. We may see food as good, a new job as good or money as good. In fact, in and of themselves, these things are good. The problem is that it is possible to become attached to these or any goods in a disordered and, therefore, sinful way.

For example, if someone robs a bank, they most likely do so because they are seeing the result of their robbery – money – as something good. Money, in and of itself, is a good. There is nothing wrong with it. But it is possible to desire money in a disordered way. In that case, the disordered attachment to money may lead a person to choose money over the moral truth that we should not steal. They choose to steal because their conscience is confused and erroneously sees the money as the greater good. This is the result of an unhealthy attachment to money.

The same could be said of food. Food is good in and of itself. But when one desires it to a serious and disordered degree, food can lead one to gluttony. Thus, the excessive attachment to food is sinful.

Sin destroys our happiness when it causes us to become attached to goods we desire in a disordered way. But, interestingly, no one chooses to excessively become attached to something so that they can become miserable. Sure, they may realize this fact in the back of their minds, but it would be rarely the case that someone chooses a disordered attachment to something because they know it's wrong. They choose it because they are deceived and confused and have allowed their will to become weakened and controlled, or even addicted.

Descriptions of Sin: Sin has traditionally been categorized in various ways. Below are some of the most common categories.

Spiritual Sins: These are the worst of sins and do the most damage. They are sins such as pride (self-centeredness), blasphemy (disrespect toward God or His Church) and apostasy (the direct denial of faith).

Carnal Sins: These are sins of the flesh. Galatians 5:19-21 outlines the sins of the flesh: "Now the works of the flesh are obvious: immorality, impurity, licentiousness, idolatry, sorcery, hatreds, rivalry, jealousy, outbursts of fury, acts of selfishness, dissensions, factions, occasions of envy, drinking bouts, orgies, and the like."

Sins of Commission vs. Omission: The more serious sins we have are most often the things we actively and intentionally do: sins of commission. We commit an offense against God or our neighbor. But there are also sins of "omission" meaning that we failed to do something we should. We failed in virtue, mercy, kindness, or the like. This is neglect on our part and is still sin.

Spiritual Imperfections: Related to sins of omission are spiritual imperfections. These are sins that are simply a lacking of perfect love. They are still sin but are more in the realm of a lack of perfect love rather than something we actively do. We will always find spiritual imperfections in our life, especially a lacking of perfect faith, hope and charity.

Sins Against Virtue: Another distinction we can make regarding sin are those ways we fail to live virtue to perfection. A virtue is usually defined as "the means between the extremes." Therefore, if we are excessive or lacking in an area of our life, we are most likely lacking in virtue. This lack of virtue is also a form of sin.

Object of Sin: There are traditionally three objects of our sin: God, neighbor or self. We can sin directly against God through disobedience and other spiritual sins. We sin against our neighbor with any lack of charity. But we can also sin against ourselves, or with ourselves by sins such as gluttony, masturbation, self-pity, etc. Understanding the three possible objects of sin is of great benefit in overcoming sin.

Mortal vs. Venial: The most common distinction in sin is moral versus venial. More will be said on this below but, for now, suffice it to say that moral sin refers to sins of the most serious nature which completely cut off our relationship with God. Venial sins refer to every other type of sin that fails to reach the ultimate level of being mortal.

Thought, Word or Deed: A final traditional distinction is to identify where the sin resides. We can sin simply in our thoughts. Thoughts can then, also, turn into sins in our words or in our actions. Again, it's helpful to be able to identify which type of sin we have.

Gravity of Sin

The most common distinction we make in sin is that of mortal vs. venial. It's important to know the difference and the effects that each type of sin has on us. It's also important to know the difference so that we know how to overcome each form of these sins.

Venial Sin: Venial sin is basically every sin that fails to rise to the grave level of mortal sin. If it is sin and is not mortal, then it's venial. Venial sins can be sins of commission or sins of omission. They can also be spiritual imperfections. The best way to understand venial sin is to look at it in the light of mortal sin. Again, if our sin is not mortal, then it falls to the level of venial.

Venial sins do not have the power to completely sever our relationship with God. But they do have the effect of harming our relationship with God and doing damage to our own soul. Venial sins can build upon themselves leading to other venial sins. However, a thousand venial sins can never equal a mortal sin. A mortal sin is of a completely different category. With that said, it's also important to note that venial sins, especially when they grow in number, can weaken us such that we are more likely to commit a mortal sin.

Venial sins are forgiven in Confession but can also be forgiven through prayer, by receiving Holy Communion and through a good act of contrition. But Confession is the ideal place to receive forgiveness for venial sins since this Sacrament adds a special grace to the area we need it the most.

Mortal Sin: Mortal sin is the most serious sin and its effect is to be understood by its very name: mortal. Mortal means deadly and, therefore, mortal sin completely kills the grace of God in our heart. It leaves us spiritually dead and lacking in charity and hope.

Interestingly, mortal sin does not necessarily destroy faith in our lives. It certainly attacks our faith and confuses it, but faith is still possible while in mortal sin. In fact, it is that enduring ability to have faith that can have the effect of enabling one to repent of mortal sin and return to God.

However, even though faith is not necessarily completely destroyed by mortal sin, hope and charity are. The soul in unrepentant mortal sin is not able to hope in God in any way and is not capable of offering the charity which results from sanctifying grace.

Understanding mortal sin can seem a bit technical and hard to understand on a practical level. Nonetheless, it's important to understand the nature of mortal sin (as explained above) as well as the conditions of committing a mortal sin. The conditions are as follows:

Grave Matter: For a sin to be mortal, the first condition is that the action done is grave. This can be hard to distinguish at times for some sins, but other sins are clear. Any grave violation of the Ten Commandments should be considered grave matter. Here are some obvious examples: Murder, violence, arson, theft, adultery, fornication, abortion, blasphemy, apostasy, etc. These are some of the most grievous acts one can commit. It's true that all of these actions can be done to a lesser degree, but for them to be grave we should think of these actions being done to the most serious degree.

Full Knowledge: A second necessary condition of mortal sin is that one performs the grave act with full knowledge that it is gravely wrong. Note that the word "full" is used here to qualify one's knowledge. It's not just a matter of suspecting it's wrong or even being pretty certain; rather, there must be a complete understanding of the seriousness and gravity of the action. "Full" means 100%. God knows if we know the gravity of the sin and He knows if we are ignorant. Hopefully, if we are honest with ourselves, we will also be able to admit to the depth of our knowledge and admit when we do in fact have full knowledge.

Complete Consent: Again, note here the use of the word "complete" to qualify the type of consent given. It's not enough to simply do the action; it must also be done in a completely free way by one's own free will. Complete, once again, means done freely with 100% of your free will. Anything less than 100% does not meet the requirement of mortal sin.

With a basic understanding of these three conditions of mortal sin, we can also see that any lacking in one of these three conditions immediately lessens the personal responsibility one may have and, thus, the sin only becomes venial. It doesn't mean that the sin is any less wrong, it just means we may not be as personally responsible for what we have done and, thus, we may not have completely, 100%, cut off our relationship with God.

For now it is sufficient to understand these basic principles of sin. Later in this book, when we look at specific sins, we will use these three conditions to help highlight the more practical difference between mortal and venial sin.

2

THE LAW, SOCIETY, GRACE AND SALVATION

So do you want to obtain a life of beatitude? That is, a life of true blessedness? A life of true happiness? Of course you do! The more important question is, "How do I obtain it?"

The answer is simple. We obtain it through the divine help of Christ. And how does He help us? He helps us, 1) through the law, and 2) through grace.

This chapter will focus in on the way God has given us His *law*, as well as the way He gives us *grace* so as to live the glorious life we are called to live.

The Moral Law

The "moral law" is also to be understood as the "divine law." The divine law is everything that comes from the mind and heart of God as right and good. It is the moral order that God has established to guide us into a life of fulfillment. By analogy, we understand that there are laws of nature. Gravity, for example, cannot be ignored. We may be able to pretend it doesn't exist, but that does not mean it does not exist. So it is with the moral (divine) law of God. This spiritual law is real and unchanging. Denying it does not make it disappear.

This law should be first understood as something that is rational. It makes sense. This is the case because God made us with an innate ability to comprehend right from wrong. We may not be able to discern every moral law from God through our human reason alone, but we will be able to understand the most basic laws of morality through our reason and common sense. That's because the moral law is written upon our conscience.

With that said, it's important to understand that even those laws of the highest order (such as "love your enemies") do make sense to us when we let God reveal them to us in the ways He chooses. The bottom line is that the moral law makes sense!

When speaking of the moral law (divine law) we define four manifestations of it: natural law, revealed law, ecclesiastical laws and civil laws. We'll look at each one so as to understand how God has chosen to guide us toward beatitude.

Natural Law: The natural law is a law of morality written upon the conscience of every person. It's a law of morality that we simply know by nature. This law, acting in accord with human reason, calls us to do good and forbids us to sin. There are two key aspects of the natural law we see in this definition. First, the natural law is "engraved in the soul of each and every man," and, second, this law calls man "to do good and forbidding him to sin" (*CCC* #1954).

Think about your knowledge of right and wrong. Where did it come from? Is it purely the result of what you've been taught by parents and others throughout your life? Or is there a source that goes beyond that which you were taught? The truth is that there are many things we simply know to be good and other things we know to be wrong. This is because God has written His law upon our human reason.

For example, why do you know it's wrong to kill someone? Or why do you know it's wrong to steal a large sum of money from a neighbor? Is it only because you were taught this way? No, there is more to it. It's true that being taught right from wrong helps us, but deep down we do know certain basic moral principles. We know them because we have to know them. And we have to know them because God has made His law part of our very nature.

The problem is that our human nature is "messed up" so to speak. We have been greatly affected by Original Sin and what we call "concupiscence." This means that our very nature is distorted and disordered. As a result, that law of God written upon our conscience is blurred and confused. If we had a perfect human nature all would be clear, but we don't and, therefore, the natural law is confused at times. But with that said, if we try to seek the truth within our human reason, we will at very least arrive at the most basic of moral principles and will be able to be guided by them. And, as explained above, ignoring the natural moral law does not make it go away.

Revealed Law: We spoke in Book One of this series about revelation. In that book we primarily dealt with matters of <u>faith</u>. Here, we follow the same understanding but look at revelation regarding matters of <u>morality</u>.

As explained above, the natural law given to us by God and inscribed on our very conscience is somewhat confused as a result of Original Sin and our personal sins. It's not that the law itself is confused; rather, it's that our ability to comprehend the law of God is made difficult because of our fallen state. But God did not leave us in our confusion. Instead, He began from the beginning of time to reveal to us the full moral law so as to clarify that which we struggle with.

In the Old Testament we see that God began to reveal His law as early as Adam and Eve and continued to reveal His law to those who came after. This was done with Noah, Abraham and especially through Moses when God gave him the Ten Commandments. We see the continuing revelation of God regarding morality in the teaching of the prophets, the development of the Old Testament Law and in the many ways in which God interacted with His people.

Ultimately, The Father revealed the fullness of the moral law to us in His Son, Jesus. Jesus, in His teaching and in His very person and actions, reveals the fullness of what it means to be human and to embrace the perfect law of love.

Without this revelation of God we would remain in darkness and confusion. But with this revelation of God we are given the ability to see clearly all that God has established as good, holy and morally upright.

This is seen most clearly when we read the Scriptures, especially the Gospels. When we read the words of Jesus, in particular, we may sit back and be convicted in one way or another on how we have been acting poorly or ways in which we need to improve. This is good! When this happens we are letting the deep revelation of God penetrate our consciences and teach us how to act. We may feel "convicted" in the sense that we suddenly realize we have been less than perfect in some area of our life. And we may find, in the Scriptures, a deep calling to work toward more perfect virtue and love.

What's interesting is that the law of love may, at first, feel like a burden or challenge to us. Or, it may be hard to accept and embrace. But, in the end, if we are open and sincerely seek the truth, we will come to realize that all Jesus says and does makes sense. It's like a key opening a locked door to a world we had heard about but could not discover on our own. The revelations Jesus gives us are purifying and freeing to us because they reveal to us what is already hidden within our conscience. They reveal the moral law inscribed within us and it becomes a joyful discovery.

The law that the Gospels reveal is the law of charity. This law is especially found in the Beatitudes and the Sermon on the Mount. But we also see this law of charity in the ultimate sacrificial act of love that Jesus offered on the Cross. We read His words and see His free embrace of this sacrifice for us. In the witness of His Cross we discover our own calling of sacrificial love and hopefully embrace it wholeheartedly.

Ecclesiastical Law: When Jesus ascended into Heaven He promised He would be with us always. The primary way this happens is through the Church. The Church, in the persons of the Apostles and their successors, is entrusted with the "Keys to the Kingdom." This means that Jesus promises to lead us into all truth throughout time.

It's the sacred role of the Church, especially the pope and bishops, to teach on matters of faith and morals throughout time. This is especially important as new moral questions arise in each day and age. It may be good to refer to the section on the Magisterium in Book One of this series for a clearer explanation. All that is said there refers, especially, to the way that God guides the Church in the ways of faith. However, the teaching authority of the Magisterium also equally applies to all matters of the moral life. It is the role of the Magisterium to teach and clarify the moral law for us in every day and age.

For example, Jesus never taught us about the morality of cloning or embryonic stem cell research. Therefore, it's the responsibility of the Church to take the moral clarity given through the teaching of Jesus and apply it to all modern questions. Therefore, we can be certain that Jesus brings clarity to His revelation as new questions arise.

The Church is also given the authority and, therefore, the responsibility, to offer laws to guide our worship and life of faith. For example, the teaching on attending Mass on holy days of obligation is a divine law that is taught through the Church. It is a particular way in which we honor and keep the Third Commandment. Jesus wants us to be obedient to these laws.

Ecclesiastical laws govern the celebration of the Sacraments, the organization of parishes and dioceses, guide the responsibility of bishops and pastors, help those called to religious life, etc. The Church gives us what we call Canon Law to guide most parts of our activities but there are also many other ways in which Church laws guide us. There are particular laws set up in each local church, diocese and country. There are laws that apply to each religious community and organization. There are more universal liturgical laws. And there are other moral laws taught by the Church. One specific ecclesiastical law given to us is called the Precepts of the Church. These precepts are as follows:

1. Attend Mass on Sundays and holy days of obligation.
2. Confess your sins at least once a year.
3. Receive Holy Communion at least during the Easter season.
4. Keep holy the holy days of obligation.
5. Observe the prescribed days of fasting and abstinence.

Additionally, the faithful have the duty of providing for the material needs of the Church, each according to his abilities.

These precepts are ecclesiastical laws that provide us with what we may call the "minimum requirements" for each person to grow in holiness and the moral life. These ecclesiastical laws are in perfect conformity with the divine law of God but are particular ways in which God manifests His law to us through the Church.

Civil Law: Civil laws are to be followed when they are in union with the mind and will of God. When a civil law is enacted by a legitimate authority for the common good of the people, it is a participation in the Divine Law of God and must be followed. However, if a civil law is in clear contradiction to the Divine Law, and therefore, contrary to our human reason, we are obliged not to follow it.

As a way of understanding how the moral law should work hand-in-hand with civil law and the common good of society, the next section looks more clearly at the way God's law affects us as a human family.

Who are We? Human Society

Human beings are made for love of one another. We are made to be in communion with each other especially within our families, but also within society as a whole. The social nature of humanity goes to the heart of who we are. We are social beings and, as a result, our lives must reflect communion and union with each other. Let's look at the moral obligations of individuals, the family, the State, and all social organizations so as to understand the social nature we have been endowed with by our Creator.

The Trinity as the Basis of Society

> There is a certain resemblance between the unity of the divine persons and the fraternity that men ought to establish among themselves. (*CCC* #1890)

This short line reveals what human society is all about. To understand the nature of the person, family and all of society we need to first turn to the Trinity. The Trinity is, by its very nature, a family. It's a communion of divine Persons who live in perfect union and love with each other. So it's fair to say that community is a part of the essential nature of God. Each Person in the Trinity exists to be in union with others.

Starting with the Trinity, we have insights into our own lives, our own nature, and society as a whole. We are made in the image and likeness of God and, therefore, are made to share in His very life. We are also made for communion not only with the Trinity, but also with one another. And this communion must be made manifest in all of society. Society is a sort of training ground for each person to become more human, so to speak. Since we are made for communion with each other, the more we engage with family, friends and society as a whole, the more we discover and fulfill our human lives.

Society, on its part, must also respect the dignity of each person and realize that the human person is the central focus of society. Society must never trump the rights of the individual. Rather, the respect for the individual person is what makes society as a whole flourish as a place of human communion.

One basic principle that a society must follow is the principle of subsidiarity. This principle means that what can be handled on a personal level, should be handled on that level. What can be handled on a family, local, or State level should be handled there. In other words, society should take care not to interfere and infringe on the individual rights of its people. Big government should not try to micromanage the individual when the individual or local government can take care of the question at hand. Communism and other forms of Socialism are examples of the State taking on "rights" that belong to the individual or local community.

It's also important that individuals seek to transform society into the image of the Holy Trinity. We must strive to bring forth justice and harmony, but it must always be done in charity and truth.

Common Good

The first thing to understand about the common good has to do with legitimate authority in society. Authority is necessary and is a way for society, as a whole, to be directed by God and God's law. Those in authority are always required to respect the moral law as well as the dignity and rights of each individual.

The goal of anyone in authority is to enact only those laws which are necessary, are reasonable and are for the good of the individual and, therefore, are for the good of all. An unjust law is one which is contrary to human reason and, therefore, contrary to God's law. These laws do not have to be followed and, at times, they must be disobeyed.

For example, say a government makes a law that every family can only have one child and, if they get pregnant with a second child, that child must be aborted. This is a grave injustice and must be disobeyed regardless of the consequences. Humanity must reasonably and charitably oppose injustice like this. Civil laws that infringe on the rights and dignity of the individual never help the common good.

With that said, legitimate authority can enact laws for the common good which are reasonable. In that case, the *Catechism* identifies three qualities of the common good that will be taken into consideration:

1. As mentioned above, the common good, and all laws that are established in support of the common good, will always respect the rights and dignity of the individual. Of great importance is the respect for each person's right to act in accord with their moral conscience. Each person, for example, must be free to worship, live their vocation in faith, and enjoy their right to privacy.

2. Each individual must be given the freedom to work toward the healthy development of a society and, in the development of society, should be free to pursue those things that are fundamental needs: "food, clothing, health, work, education and culture, suitable information, the right to establish a family, and so on" (GS 26 § 2). (*CCC* #1908)

3. It is the duty of civil authority to strive to create a community of peace. Freedom from all oppression and defense of each society are serious responsibilities entrusted to those in authority. Each society must be safeguarded and protected from foreign and domestic oppression, violence and dominance.

There are various ways in which political structures can be set up, but whatever the structure may be, the basic rights of all must be respected. Only by this respect for the person will a society truly thrive and create an environment in which humanity can prosper in the truest sense of the word.

With the above understanding of the moral law and the way in which that moral law is made manifest in various other forms of law, we will now turn to the more supernatural end of all law by looking at the goal of humanity. We are called to live in the grace of God and, in that grace, live lives that are fully human.

Justification

Our ultimate goal in the moral life is justification. What is justification? It means two basic things. First, it means that the Holy Spirit draws us into the death and resurrection of Christ thus freeing us from sin and death. Secondly, it also means that we are inwardly transformed and renewed in Christ. We are converted to a new life in Christ, made holy and live as a new creation. Forgiveness is the first step, new life in Christ by an inward transformation is the ultimate goal.

St. Augustine is quoted in the *Catechism* as saying, "the justification of the wicked is a greater work than the creation of heaven and earth," because "heaven and earth will pass away but the salvation and justification of the elect... will not pass away" (St. Augustine, In Jo. ev. 72, 3: PL 35, 1823). (#1994)

Justification is righteousness. We are made righteous in that we are purified from all sin by the blood of Christ. And from there we are elevated to a new life of being righteous before the Father. This is not the result of our own merit; rather, it's the result of the merits of Christ's sacrifice which makes us true sons and daughters of God.

Grace

Grace is the name for every way that God pours forth His gifts of love, mercy, and holiness upon our souls. It leads us to repentance, brings forgiveness, enables us to live a life of holiness and helps us live our calling and vocation in Christ. There are various distinctions we make when speaking of grace.

Actual Grace: An actual grace is the term used for those promptings from God to call us to a life of conversion and holiness. It's the initial gift God gives to draw us in. These graces are not something we have earned or have a right to; rather, they are free gifts from God given out of love for us.

You may experience an actual grace, for example, when God speaks to your conscience revealing that you have sinned and need to return to Him. It may also come in the form of an inspiration to pray or read the

Scriptures. It could be a grace given to encourage you to reconcile with someone or offer mercy and love.

Sanctifying Grace: "Sanctity" means "holiness." Sanctifying grace is the term we use to refer to the permanent and ongoing presence of God in your life helping you to remain holy and live according to His will. When one is in a state of sanctifying grace, they are on their way to Heaven. All Christians are called to live habitually in sanctifying grace. To lose sanctifying grace one must commit a mortal sin. In that case, all sanctifying grace is lost and one may then be in need of a new actual grace to be called back to Christ.

Sanctifying grace is given in Baptism and remains as long as the person remains faithful to the will of God. This grace, therefore, is what makes us holy and just before God. If you are in a state of sanctifying grace, you are living in a relationship with Christ. He is alive within you and you are living in Him. Sanctifying grace comes to us in varying degrees. The greatest of saints are consumed by this grace and led by it in all their actions. That person one step away from mortal sin is also in sanctifying grace, but to a much lesser degree.

Sacramental Grace: This is a term used to specify the grace given to us through the Sacraments. It's first given in Baptism and is subsequently given through our participation in every other Sacrament. Sacramental graces have the goal of enabling us to permanently live in sanctifying grace and, in fact, produce sanctifying grace in our lives. The only distinction here is that sacramental grace is sanctifying grace that comes to us through the Sacraments.

Special Graces: These graces are given in various forms of charisms. A charism is a special gift of God given to a person so as to build up the Church and fulfill a mission for the good of others. These charisms could be mysterious in the sense of being an ability to prophesy, speak in tongues, or perform miracles. They can also be special gifts given to enable one to be good administrators within the Church or perform other special functions proper to one's vocation such as being a dedicated mom or dad. A charism is given always for the good of others.

Merit

In Matthew's Gospel we read:

> Do not store up for yourselves treasures on earth, where moth and decay destroy, and thieves break in and steal. But store up treasures in heaven, where neither moth nor decay destroys, nor thieves break in and steal. (Matthew 6:19-20)

How do we "store up treasure in Heaven?" Truth be told, we cannot do this by ourselves and have no right, whatsoever, to treasure or riches in Heaven. This is an important foundational starting point to begin with if we are to understand merit.

Merit can be seen as that which is owed someone first by the community. If we do evil, we merit rebuke and punishment from others. If we do good, we merit their praise and gratitude.

Regarding God, we can do nothing to deserve His gratitude and praise. Why? Because everything good is a gift from God. All is gift! For that reason, we must be careful with the term "merit" lest we think we can earn our salvation or any reward or blessing from God. We cannot.

However, God is so good that He wills to reward us for our cooperation with His divine plan and grace. Therefore, by God's will, every time we serve Him faithfully and willfully, God sees this and rewards it with His blessings. He freely chooses to bestow eternal blessings on us, treasures in Heaven, because of His love and mercy.

This should especially address, for us, the importance of getting holy now rather than waiting until our time of death. Sure, a deathbed conversion is honored by God, but what is far better is a life-long commitment to holiness and conversion. In this case, our life of holiness continually invites God to act in a free and gratuitous way in which He bestows eternal treasures upon us. Our God is abundant in His generosity and He wants to bestow His generous gifts on us so that they last for eternity!

Holiness

> For those he foreknew he also predestined to be conformed to the image of his Son, so that he might be the firstborn among many brothers. And those he predestined he also called; and those he called he also justified; and those he justified he also glorified. (Rom 8:29-30)

This passage, from St. Paul, reveals our calling to holiness. The whole goal of the moral life is to obtain Christian holiness. We are called to become conformed to the image of Christ and, in that, to be justified and glorified.

Sometimes we can think that great holiness is something only for the saints, or for priests and religious. But it's essential to know and believe that every one of us is called to holiness. Moms and dads must become holy parents. Children must be holy. Married, single, religious and priests are called to obtain holiness. Holiness is synonymous with true happiness. It's easy to forget that. Sometimes we can think that holiness means we live a boring and difficult life. That's true if the measure of happiness is from a worldly and secular perspective. Worldly happiness is temporary, passing and very superficial. If, however, we understand happiness from the perspective of the truth of who we are and what we are made for, we will realize that happiness is holiness. And holiness means a life filled with the grace of God, calling us to a deeper conversion, and enabling us to grow in our interior conversion each and every day. This interior world of grace and holiness is the key to discovering and becoming who we are and what we are made for.

From the Speculative to the Practical

The moral principles outlined in this and the previous chapter must be first understood in a more speculative way. They must be understood as the general guiding foundation of morality. But the purpose of that is so that they can then move to the practical part of our life. We must be able to take the principles we know and apply them to daily life. Without this, the moral principles remain just theoretical principles we can discuss in a theoretical way.

The way they become practical is by applying them to daily life and daily decisions we face. This is best done by looking at the clearest and most practical moral revelation we have been given by God: the Ten Commandments.

The Ten Commandments are the clear revelation of God's law and provide us with the framework for how we are to live. Each Commandment covers a broad spectrum in that they provide us with a bottom line of what not to do, but also an upper limit of what holy living is all about.

As we go through each commandment and, thus, as we reflect upon the entirety of the moral law of God, try to see how the moral principles already discussed are made concrete and practical. And try to use the following reflections on the Commandments as a source of your own moral living.

3

LOVING GOD

The First Commandment:

> I am the LORD your God, who brought you out of the land of Egypt, out of the house of slavery. You shall not have other gods beside me. You shall not make for yourself an idol or a likeness of anything in the heavens above or on the earth below or in the waters beneath the earth; you shall not bow down before them or serve them. (Exodus 20:2-5)

> It is written: "The Lord, your God, shall you worship and him alone shall you serve." (Matthew 4:10)

Do you love God? Certainly you do! But this is not just a black and white question. It's not as if the answer is either yes or no and that's it. Love of God must be lived on many levels and in many ways and must continually grow deeper. Ultimately, love of God calls us to be a total gift of ourselves to God, making Him the center of our lives.

The First Commandment calls us to know God, love Him and worship Him above all else. The "bottom line" of this Commandment is that we should not worship false gods, but the upper limit is to offer the worship and love we owe God because of who He is, and to do this in an unconditional and unlimited way. Let's begin by looking at the bottom line and upper limit in more detail.

Our High Calling of Love

Morality is often seen only in a negative way. We see what we should not do. But it's important that we move beyond seeing morality in only a negative way by looking to what morality is in a positive light.

Serving God and loving Him above all things means there are many glorious and positive things we are called to. Here are a few of the high callings we receive from this Commandment.

Adoration: To adore God is one of our highest callings. Surprisingly, it means we first recognize our nothingness before God. Yes, that's right, nothingness! This is the heart and soul of humility. We are weak and without God we are nothing. Our pride can make this hard to admit. But when we can recognize this, adoration then enables us to offer all glory to God rather than ourselves. It enables us to bow down before Him in love and worship as we offer all the praise and glory to Him.

Prayer: We are called to "pray always." By making God the center of our lives, we choose, also, to make prayer the center of our lives. Prayer is the active way in which we unite ourselves to God making Him the center of our lives.

Sacrifice: At the heart of love is sacrifice. Sacrifice, on a secular and superficial level, does not make sense. But on a spiritual level of faith, sacrifice is one of our greatest joys. Sacrifice is at the heart of the love of Jesus in that He willingly gave His life on the Cross so as to atone for our sins. Sacrifice, on our part, must not be seen in a negative light. Rather, sacrifice must be seen as a wonderful opportunity to put God and His will first in our lives. To live a sacrificial life is nothing other than to make the will of God more important than anything else in our lives. The fruit of sacrifice is spiritual joy and peace, knowing that we are achieving the reason for our existence.

Promises and Vows: There are various times when we are called to show honor and respect to God through solemn promises and vows. These public commitments to God are made in the various sacraments such as Baptism, Confirmation, Marriage and Holy Orders. Making a promise or vow to God and then fulfilling it is a duty of every Christian. Some are called to unique expressions of vows in the religious life offering chastity, obedience and poverty to God in a solemn way.

Additionally, Christians may make personal promises to God as a way of entrusting themselves to Him and relying upon His grace to fulfill that promise. Promises on this level are personal manifestations of faith.

Religious Liberty: This Commandment demands that society as a whole and, more specifically, those entrusted with civil authority respect the rights of each person to worship God and live out their faith. We must be free to act in accord with our conscience and be free to live out God's will in our lives.

The Bottom Line of This Commandment

In addition to calling us to a life of worship that makes God the center of our lives, this Commandment forbids certain acts also. Below is a list of some of the things forbidden.

Superstition: This is the act of attributing some "magical" power to an action, ritual or item. At times, Christians can even exaggerate certain good acts of piety attributing to those acts of devotion a power that should be attributed to God alone. For example, novenas are wonderful forms of prayer which often have as their goal the seeking of spiritual graces. However, there are times when novenas or other pious acts are presented in such a way that we are led to believe that if we say certain prayers in a certain way, we are guaranteed God will answer whatever we request. In this case there can be a danger of turning a holy and pious act into a superstitious one.

Idolatry: Idolatry is a way of treating something other than God as a god. Obviously acts of pagan worship or Satanism are examples of this. However, the *Catechism* points out that we can also make a god out of "power, pleasure, race, ancestors, the state, money, etc." (#2113).

Divination and Magic: The *Catechism* points out that seeking spiritual power from a source other than God contradicts this Commandment in these and other ways: "recourse to Satan or demons, conjuring up the dead or other practices that falsely try to 'unveil' the future. Consulting horoscopes, astrology, palm reading, interpretation of omens and lots, the phenomena of clairvoyance, and recourse to mediums" (#2116) are all violations of this Commandment.

Irreligion: "God's first Commandment condemns the main sins of irreligion: tempting God, in words or deeds, sacrilege, and simony" (*CCC* #2118). Tempting God is a way of testing or challenging Him to act in accord with our will or to tempt Him to manifest His power. We cannot tempt God, but we can try to manipulate Him. And trying this is a sin of irreligion.

A sacrilege is also an act of irreligion. It is an act or word by which we treat something sacred in a profane way. This is especially true of the Sacraments. An obvious and very serious example of this would be the desecration of the Holy Eucharist. We can also commit a sacrilege by treating a person in a profane way.

Simony is an attempt to put a price on sacred things by trying to buy spiritual graces. It is named after the magician Simon Magus from the story of Acts 8:9-24. In that story, Peter and John were praying over the newly baptized and bestowing the Holy Spirit upon them. When Simon saw this he offered them money so that he, too, could have this power of bestowing the Holy Spirit. He was harshly chastised by Peter and he repented.

Atheism: Perhaps this sin is the most obvious violation of the First Commandment. Atheism is a direct denial of God and a rejection of all He has revealed. It's a refusal to have faith.

Agnosticism: One step down from atheism is agnosticism. The agnostic holds the conviction that God is uncertain and that they do not know if there is a god. This can come in the form of a direct refusal to make any act of faith, indifferentism, or laziness in the area of faith. Some agnostics may actually be searching for God; others may not and, thus, can be considered practical atheists.

Graven Images

This Commandment obviously prohibits the making of a false god and treating it as God. The story of the golden calf found in Exodus 32 is a good example of the direct violation of this Commandment. It should be obvious that if we create an image and attribute to that image a certain sacred power separate from the power of God, we are breaking this Commandment.

With that said, there is a long standing tradition within the Catholic Church and various other Christian Churches to honor the saints and Jesus Himself through the use of sacred art. These artistic expressions can be seen as icons of the saints, statues, stained glass, paintings, crucifixes, and the like.

From time to time there are people who challenge this practice and suggest that the practice of honoring statues and other forms of sacred art is a violation of the First Commandment. Is it?

The only way these practices would be a violation of the First Commandment is if we act as if the images of sacred art are godlike. In other words, if we believe that the piece of art in question has power in and of itself, separate from God, then this is a sin. But this is clearly not our Catholic tradition.

Because Jesus took on flesh and entered our world, the world itself is capable of reflecting God's glory. Art is one way of trying to capture and reflect that glory and beauty of God.

Sacred art offers us a source of reflection, beauty and meditation. It's a way of preaching the Gospel through signs and images. Therefore, when a person prays before a crucifix, that person is not doing so with the belief that that particular crucifix is the source of grace. That would be foolish. Rather, praying before a crucifix, or any other sacred image, is a way of using the visual world to honor the spiritual world. It's a way of transcending this world so as to connect with God who is transcendent of this world while, at the same time, He is ever present to us in this world. When sacred art is used in the right way, it helps to draw us to the divine and enter more deeply into divine realities.

The Upper Upper Limit!

To understand what we may call the "upper upper limit" of this Commandment we must look at the wonderful theological virtues of faith, hope and charity.

Faith: We are called to have a deep faith in God. Faith in God means we know Him, believe in Him and understand Him. It means we foster a true relationship with Him so as to know Him more. When we have faith, we seek to have more. The more we know God, the more we want to know God and the more we come to know God. We are drawn, by faith, to seek Him on an ever-deepening level.

Sins against faith would include any ways that we neglect our duty to seek God and know Him. It's important to understand that we have a moral duty to seek God and to seek the truth. At times we can fail to seek God and grow in personal knowledge of Him because of laziness. At other times it can be a direct and willful indifference. Whatever the case may be, if we are negligent in our duty to seek God and to come to know Him, we break this Commandment which calls us to make Him the center of our lives.

Hope: As we come to faith in God, we will also be filled with a supernatural gift of hope. This gift of hope compels us to seek eternal salvation and to seek a life filled with the virtues God desires to bestow upon us. The upper limit and positive calling of this Commandment, in regard to divine hope, is that we remain steadfast in all that God speaks to us no matter what we go through and no matter what cross we may carry. We are compelled and strengthened to continue our pursuit of God and His holy will.

Sins against hope would include despair. When we give in to despair we give up on God and give up on His promises to us which we receive and understand through the gift of faith. Sure, despair can also be caused, at times, by more psychological factors rather than sinful or spiritual factors. But, nonetheless, despair is opposed to hope no matter how it comes after us.

Another danger that we can fall into is presumption. Presumption is a very subtle sin which manifests itself in one of two ways. First, it can manifest itself in such a way that we fall into the trap of thinking we are good enough to make it on our own. We look to ourselves, in a sense, as our own god. This is foolishness but when it happens, we believe that we can rely upon our own strength and abilities to fulfill our lives.

A second way that one can fall into presumption is to have an exaggerated view of God's mercy. True, God's mercy is perfect and always there. But some can fall into the trap of thinking that God will forgive them even though they do not repent of their sins. In other words, they do not arrive at a true sorrow for sin and, therefore, do not fully convert. As a result, they presume on God's mercy. What they fail to see is that forgiveness is dependent upon one's sorrow and willingness to change. If there is no willingness to change, mercy cannot be offered or received.

Charity: Charity is first of all love of God.   Charity is born when we first have faith in God, believe all that He reveals, and then are filled with hope in His promises.   When this happens we are moved to a deep and sustaining love of God.

To love God is to make Him and His will the center of our lives. Nothing becomes more important than God.   Sins against charity toward God would be lukewarmness, laziness, disinterest, and most certainly hatred of God.   Those who have a hatred of God would most likely be confused first in their faith.   But those who have a simple negligence, or are lukewarm, may have faith but subsequently lack the drive to live what their faith calls them to.

Practical Applications

We now can begin to take the moral principles of the first two chapters and apply them specifically to the moral laws of God.   We start with this First Commandment of the Lord.

Let's first look at ways that it is mortally broken.   Remember that in order to commit a mortal sin we need three things: 1) grave matter; 2) full knowledge; 3) complete consent of the will.

Grave Matter: What would be a <u>grave</u> violation of this Commandment?   Serious superstition, idolatry, divination, magic, atheism, agnosticism, and worshiping false images would be at the top of the list.   Any one of these acts done to a serious degree would be grave matter.

A good distinction can be found in superstition.   Say, for example, you jokingly refuse to walk under a ladder because it's "bad luck."   Well, it's not bad luck, that's just superstition.   But something as silly as this most certainly doesn't fall into the category of grave matter.   However, if you were to make someone you dislike walk under a ladder because you wholeheartedly believed that it was bad luck and you were convinced this would do them serious damage then we might start approaching superstition to a serious degree.   Perhaps a more obvious example of grave matter against the First Commandment would be divinization. Say, for example, you used the Ouija board to try to contact the dead spirits.   This is clearly grave matter.

Full Knowledge: The second requirement for this action to be mortal sin is that you fully know it's gravely wrong. So, take the person who uses the Ouija board. Let's say that on one hand you have a priest who knows all about Ouija boards, and on the other hand you have a teen that is at a sleepover and never heard of Ouija boards before. There is a clear distinction between the two. Hopefully, a priest (or anyone who fully knows Ouija boards are wrong) would never use one. But, if they did, they meet the second requirement for mortal sin. The teen that is exposed to the Ouija board for the first time may be uncertain and uninformed and, therefore, may not have full knowledge that "joining the fun" so to speak is wrong. It doesn't make this action OK, and it's still a grave violation of God's Commandment, but the teen may not be fully responsible for joining in at first.

Complete Consent of the Will: Continuing with our example, say the teen does use the Ouija board and knows it's wrong because his/her parents have carefully taught that it's wrong. There is still the question, in this case, of complete consent. Let's say that this teen has been struggling with a poor self-image after moving to a new town and new school. Say that this was the first sleepover for that teen and he/she was trying to make new friends. The Ouija board is brought out and the teen is immediately horrified but is afraid to say anything for fear of rejection. It's this teen's turn and he/she reluctantly asks a question for the board and that's it. Did that teen mortally sin? Well, it was grave matter and there was full knowledge that it was gravely wrong, but it's possible that the circumstances were such that the fear and poor self-image this teen was dealing with diminished his/her personal guilt. Again, it doesn't make those actions right, but God sees what is in the heart and will judge accordingly.

This same process of moral reasoning can be applied to any situation and to any moral law laid down by this Commandment. This shows why Chapter One and Two are so important to understand as we look at concrete moral situations that people find themselves in.

Venial Sin: As explained above, if all three conditions are met for mortal sin then the sin is mortal. However, if one or more of the conditions are not met then the sin is only venial. As far as venial sin goes, there are many levels of severity of this form of sin, but what all venial sin has in common is that it does not completely destroy our relationship with Christ.

The bottom line of venial sins would be, for example, a habitual sin of making money a "god." There may be some ways that it fails to meet the full requirement of mortal sin but, nonetheless, any willful attachment to money in an excessive way keeps us from fully turning our lives over to God.

The upper limit of venial sin may simply be a lack of full surrender to God in this area. Again, take the attachment to money. Say a person does not really have money as a god but, nonetheless, still struggles with a slight lack of complete trust in God's providential care, and therefore, worries from time to time about money. This is not serious by any means and is quite common. However, for the person who is striving for perfection, it's important to work toward a total surrender to divine providence. This means working toward a complete trust that God will provide for every need.

The Second Commandment:

> You shall not invoke the name of the LORD, your God, in vain. (Exodus 20:7)

> Again you have heard that it was said to your ancestors, "Do not take a false oath, but make good to the Lord all that you vow." But I say to you, do not swear at all. (Mt 5:33-34)

> The second commandment *prescribes respect for the Lord's name.* Like the first commandment, it belongs to the virtue of religion and more particularly it governs our use of speech in sacred matters. (*CCC* #2142).

Have you ever found it to be a strange phenomenon that when people get mad they often use God's name as a curse? This is strange to say the least. In fact, it doesn't really make much sense. Why would the name "Jesus Christ," for example, turn into an expression of frustration of anger? Even saying something like "holy cow" or the like is strange. Why would we use the word "holy" in that expression?

Perhaps it's because God's name is truly holy and worthy of great honor and respect. Therefore, in a moment of anger or frustration we are tempted to disrespect His name. This example reveals that one sin (that of anger) can lead to another.

The Bottom Line: No Swearing Allowed

The "bottom line" is that the Second Commandment forbids using God's name in a profane and blasphemous way. It forbids that we use it as a curse, a negative expression, and in any careless way. It also forbids the same improper use of the names of the saints, especially our Blessed Mother. Lastly, it forbids speaking about anything holy in a harmful or careless way. To directly criticize Christ's Church, for example, is a sin against this Commandment.

It would also be a violation of this Commandment to use God's name in making false oaths. For example, this Commandment is violated when you swear to tell the truth "so help me God" and then you lie. This is also an obvious sin against the Command "do not bear false witness." However, when God's name is invoked prior to the lie, it is a double sin. On a more casual level, it is common for someone to say something that another may not believe and then to follow that statement with, "I swear to God!" Well, even if you are telling the truth, it is careless to use God to make an oath in such a casual way about something that may not be that important.

There are times when invoking God's name under oath can be appropriate. In fact, solemn promises and vows within the Church do just that. It's more a matter of how God's name is used and in what context that determines the morality of it. Or, making a solemn promise at a civil or Church court with your hand on the Bible is appropriate, as long as you tell the whole truth.

The most important thing to remember is that invoking God's name is important. When it's done, it should be done in a holy way avoiding all carelessness and falsity.

The Upper Limit: God's Name is Holy...and so is yours!

The "upper limit" of this Commandment is that God's name is holy and should be used in the form of worship. We are to honor Him by honoring His name and using it in prayer and praise. For example, singing praises to God's name or repeating the sacred name of Jesus over and over can be a holy use of God's name.

Our prayer is another example of a holy use of God's name. We begin our prayers "In the name of the Father, and of the Son and of the Holy Spirit." This invocation of the Triune God is a way of entering into prayer. Additionally, our formal liturgical prayers often end by saying, "through our Lord Jesus Christ Your Son…" or "through Christ our Lord." In other words, we use God's name in prayer and saying His name is a form of prayer.

Another positive and holy teaching we take from this Commandment is the use of our own names and others. First of all, at Baptism every Christian is given a Christian name, or at least that's what's supposed to happen. Often times that Christian name is simply the given name of that child. But sometimes, especially in certain cultures, it is common to choose a saint name as their new Christian name. This practice reveals the sacredness of one's name and the identity that we can take in our good name. Our name is not just a name; our name cannot be separated from us. Therefore, a Christian name reveals our Christian identity.

For that reason, great care should be taken to speak well of others and never to curse them. To curse a person is to curse their name and that is a violation of this Commandment in that we are sons and daughters of God made in His image and likeness.

We should also realize that we will be marked for eternity with the name of our God. We will bear His name on our foreheads as Scripture says (Revelations 14:1).

Practical Applications

Let's, again, look at the ways that this Commandment is broken in a mortal way. From there, other practical venial violations will come clear.

Grave Matter: What are the grave ways that this Commandment is violated? As outlined above, direct cursing of God's name or God Himself is grave matter. Additionally, a serious lie under oath after invoking God's name is grave matter. Another example would be gravely cursing or harming another's name or reputation. This, also, is a grave violation of this Commandment in that each person is an image of God.

Grave violations of this Commandment diminish to venial violations when a curse or oath is of lesser importance. For example, say a person is careless in speaking ill of another by passing on some harmful information that is true, but doesn't need to be passed on. This carelessness may not rise to the grave level but is still a violation of this Commandment.

Full Knowledge: It's hard to conceive of a situation when someone does not fully know that it's wrong to speak a curse toward God. And it's hard to conceive that someone does not know that lying after invoking the name of God is wrong. But, as in the example above, it may be true that someone does not know it's wrong to curse the name of another person. A good example of this is when you curse someone who seems to "deserve it." In that case, it is conceivable that a person may actually think they are doing something OK, or even right by hurting the good name of another. They may think it's justified and this can be confusing. It's hard to sort things like this out. A good reflection for this is Jesus on the Cross. He could have spoken ill of those who crucified Him and He would have been correct in His condemnation. But what did He say? He said, "Father, forgive them, they know not what they do" (Luke 23:34). He showed great respect for them even though they didn't "deserve it."

Complete Consent of the Will: This is an aspect of this sin that is easier to understand and it is easier to see how it can diminish our personal guilt when violating this Commandment. At times, God's name is taken in vain in a moment of great emotional frustration. That does not justify it or make it right in any way. However, extreme emotion can temporarily diminish a person's personal guilt because that person may be acting out of emotion rather than full consent of the will. Another example of this is lying under oath. If a person is faced with some serious moral dilemma and they are seriously afraid of the consequences of telling the truth, they may make the poor decision to lie even if they have "sworn to God." As always, this is still wrong but the fear they face may diminish the personal guilt they have before God. Again, only God knows the heart and He will judge accordingly.

Venial Sins: If we look carefully at the descriptions above of any reduced moral responsibility we will find that many sins against this Commandment are only venial. But venial sins must be overcome so it's good to be aware of all the ways that this Commandment is broken.

The goal is to strive for the greatest virtue revealed by this Commandment. Doing that will enable a person to enter into the greatest level of respect and honor for God and others.

The Third Commandment:

> Remember the sabbath day—keep it holy. Six days you may labor and do all your work, but the seventh day is a sabbath of the LORD your God. You shall not do any work, either you, your son or your daughter, your male or female slave, your work animal, or the resident alien within your gates. (Ex 20:8-10)

> The sabbath was made for man, not man for the sabbath. That is why the Son of Man is lord even of the sabbath. (Mk 2:27-28)

The Sabbath Day after the First Creation

The Book of Genesis shares the story of God creating the world in six days and then resting on the seventh. Whether this took place in six literal days or not is unimportant to this particular discussion of the institution of the Sabbath. What is important is that this story says:

> On the seventh day God completed the work he had been doing; he rested on the seventh day from all the work he had undertaken. God blessed the seventh day and made it holy, because on it he rested from all the work he had done in creation. (Genesis 2:2-3)

So we see that from the beginning of creation, the seventh day was a special day set aside by God for rest. Interestingly, this story shows that it was first a day of rest for God. God, of course, does not need to rest literally speaking. Therefore, we need to read in this passage a revelation by God that this was not so much a day for Him to rest; rather, it was "a sabbath of solemn rest" (*CCC* #2168). The day itself is a day of rest and that affects all who share in the days God made.

In this we see that our first parents are called, also, to share in the day of rest God made. We are called to share in His creative work (the first six days) by the work and creation we are called to and capable of. But, worked into creation itself is a cycle of work and rest. We share in that cycle and should see it as essential to who we are by God's design.

The day of rest was also made holy by God. So it should not so much be seen as a day to be lazy; rather, it should be seen as a day to also be holy and enter more fully in the creative plan that we share in God's holiness.

The Sabbath, which was celebrated on Saturday, the seventh day of the week, came to be a day of spiritual "rest" in the sense of worship of God. This is especially found in the Commandment given in Deuteronomy 5:15:

> Remember that you too were once slaves in the land of Egypt, and the LORD, your God, brought you out from there with a strong hand and outstretched arm. That is why the LORD, your God, has commanded you to observe the sabbath day.

God called the Israelites to not only rest but to also celebrate the memorial of their freedom from Egypt. This was the celebration of the Passover feast. Thus, rest took on the form of worship and was an opportunity for God's people to weekly recall God's saving action as well as recommit themselves to their own fidelity to God and His covenant.

By the time that Jesus walked the Earth, the Sabbath law of rest was being abused. There was a scrupulous interpretation of how it was to be lived. Jesus, according to many of the scrupulous and judgmental scribes and Pharisees, broke the Sabbath rest on a number of occasions. For example, He was "accused" of healing people on the Sabbath which was interpreted as a form of work, thus supposedly violating the Sabbath. This, of course, is silly.

What Jesus does is give an accurate and authoritative interpretation to the Sabbath rest. He states that "The sabbath was made for man, not man for the sabbath" (Mark 2:27). He taught and witnessed that the Sabbath was primarily a day to do good and to honor God. It was a day for charity and for worship.

Worship in the New Covenant: The Eighth Day of Creation

The seventh day of creation was the day God set aside for rest and worship. But one thing that we as Christians traditionally acknowledge is that there is an "eighth day" of creation. This eighth day is the day of the new creation in Christ. It's the day of the Resurrection of Christ. For that reason, Christian Tradition has transferred the Sabbath rest to Sunday. Sunday is now the day that is to be set aside for rest, worship and charity. Among the most important things to do this day is worship God through or participation in the Most Holy Eucharist! The Eucharist is the New Passover, the New Memorial and the New Sabbath celebration. It's this day we recall the saving Sacrifice of Christ and share in that saving meal.

In addition to Sunday being the new Sabbath, the Church, in her wisdom, has instituted various holy days of obligation. These are days throughout the year when we honor some particular saving action of Christ. For example, Christmas is perhaps the most known holy day of obligation. On that day we honor the birth of Christ and we are "obliged" to share in the Holy Mass.

Here is the full list of holy days of obligation that are celebrated by the Vatican:

1. January 1: Solemnity of Mary, Mother of God
2. January 6: Epiphany
3. March 19: Solemnity of Saint Joseph, Husband of the Blessed Virgin Mary
4. Thursday of the sixth week of Easter: the Ascension
5. Thursday after Trinity Sunday: Body and Blood of Christ
6. June 29: Solemnity of Saints Peter and Paul, Apostles
7. August 15: Assumption of the Blessed Virgin Mary
8. November 1: All Saints
9. December 8: Feast of the Immaculate Conception of the Blessed Virgin Mary
10. December 25: Nativity of our Lord Jesus Christ (Christmas)

Note that I said the list above is the list of holy days of obligation celebrated in <u>Vatican City</u>. Get ready for what may at first seem confusing! The reason for this distinction is that the Church law (Canon Law) has given permission to each conference of bishops throughout the world to determine which days remain days of "obligation" for their territory.

For example, here are the ways that the bishops of the United States have set things up:

The three holy days of obligation that never change:

1. January 1: Solemnity of Mary, Mother of God
2. December 8: Feast of the Immaculate Conception of the Blessed Virgin Mary
3. December 25: Nativity of our Lord Jesus Christ (Christmas)

These two solemnities are celebrated but are permanently transferred to the following Sunday:

4. January 6: Epiphany
5. Thursday of the sixth week of Easter: the Ascension

The following is transferred to the following Sunday in most dioceses of the United States:

6. Thursday after Trinity Sunday: Body and Blood of Christ

The next two are always celebrated as solemnities but are not considered days of "obligation" when they fall on a Saturday or Monday in the United States:

7. August 15: Assumption of the Blessed Virgin Mary
8. November 1: All Saints

Finally, in the United States, the following two solemnities are still solemnities but are never days of "obligation."

9. March 19: Solemnity of Saint Joseph, Husband of the Blessed Virgin Mary
10. June 29: Solemnity of Saints Peter and Paul, Apostles

Every conference of bishops for each country/territory differs in regard to which holy days are days of obligation and which are not. The key is to check with your local diocese.

This may raise a question: "Why is it a sin to miss Mass in one place and not another?" Good question! This confuses many especially with the practice of not requiring Mass attendance for some holy days when they fall on Monday or Saturday. The simple and clear answer is that Jesus did give His Church the authority to determine the ways we worship. The universal Church (the pope) has, in turn, passed that authority on to the conferences of bishops and some of those conferences of bishops have even, in turn, passed that authority on to the local dioceses and provinces.

The bottom line is that we are obliged to worship God by our participation in the Holy Mass on the designated days as designated by either the universal or local Church. The upper limit is that we are privileged beyond belief to enter into worship of God and celebrate particular aspects of our faith throughout the year.

Rest in the New Covenant: The Eighth Day of Creation

A last point to make is that of rest on Sundays. The Sunday rest should not be interpreted in the scrupulous way that the Pharisees interpreted it. Rather, it should be seen in the following ways:

Works of Charity: In addition to worship of God on Sundays, care should be taken to look for opportunities to perform charitable works on Sunday. A good example of this was found at a holy convent founded by Blessed Mother Teresa. One day someone saw the sisters planting flowers before a statue of the Blessed Mother on Sunday. He said, "Sisters, you're not supposed to work on Sundays." The sisters responded, "Oh, this is not work, this is an act of love for our Blessed Mother." With that they smiled and continued their act of love.

Works of Leisure: In addition to works of charity, works of leisure are appropriate for Sunday. A work of leisure would be any activity that is truly enjoyed or experienced as refreshing. Hobbies, gardening (if it's enjoyed), family fun, cooking, etc. could all fall into this category. The key is that it is refreshing and restful for the person. Holy leisure is a way of continuing the creation for God with recreation (or re-creation).

Necessary Service: Some people simply do have to work on Sunday as a way of contributing to the common good or the rest and leisure of others. Obvious examples would be police officers, doctors, and firefighters. However, there are other works that can be permitted for the good relaxation of others and to provide basic needs. For example, gas stations can legitimately be open (people need gas to get to church!), restaurants can serve people who wish to relax with a nice dinner, and there are a variety of other similar needs that must be met. The bottom line is that we should be prudent and honest as to whether or not this is a good and necessary work that offers a needed or beneficial service to others on their day of rest.

With that said, for those who do need to work on Sundays for the good of society, it is essential that they be allowed to worship and also have suitable time off during other days of the week so as to find the necessary rest God desires for them. We live in a busy world today and that world needs to do a better job of allowing its citizens to take care of themselves and their families.

Duties of Society

One last important point to make is that the whole of society has a duty to foster the ability of Christians to honor the Lord's Day. Government, businesses, civic organizations and the like have a duty to respect the religious liberty of all so that they can worship, rest and offer charity on the Lord's Day. Employers must not impose strict requirements that hinder Sunday worship. Social organizations must see Sunday as a day for worship and family. The Government should recognize the importance of this day in the lives of its citizens and offer the proper respect for that day.

Over the past thirty years many cultures have seen a shift in the way that Sunday, in particular, is honored. Slowly, businesses began opening which imposed the burden of unnecessary work on many. Various social activities have begun to take away from healthy family life. And Sunday worship, for many, is now being crowded by numerous expectations. Life is getting busier for many as a result and this hurts the ability for many, especially families, to properly honor the Lord's Day.

One obligation that we, as citizens, have toward society is to refrain from fostering the secularization of the Lord's Day. One example of a particular way this can be done is to refrain from unnecessary shopping on Sunday. Many stores (most of them) do not need to be open on Sundays. However, they are open because people use them. It should be seen as the duty of every Christian to help reclaim the holiness of the Lord's Day by refusing to participate in unnecessary shopping and the like. It's true that there will always be exceptions that may be judged as appropriate, but the general rule should still apply. One example of a general exception could be as follows. Say you are having a family gathering and as you are preparing the meal you realize you forgot an essential ingredient. You do not support the idea of stores being open on Sundays but you know that the one up the road is open. Is it permissible to go buy that essential ingredient? Most likely the answer is "yes." In the end, it's a matter of making a good judgment of prudence.

Practical Considerations

It's hard to clearly identify the specific ways that this Commandment could end in mortal sin. However, as a way of understanding the various conditions of sin, and especially mortal sin, let's look at some specific examples.

Grave Matter: In what ways could this Commandment be violated to a serious extent? What would be considered a grave violation of this Commandment? First and foremost the most obvious serious violation of this Commandment would be missing Sunday Mass and/or missing Mass on holy days of obligation. The requirement to worship God on these days is of utmost importance and any way that someone fails to fulfill this requirement is a direct and serious violation of this Commandment.

Additionally, it could be serious if someone ignores the aspect of rest to a serious degree. For example, if someone completely neglects the Sabbath rest and, instead, chooses to engage in unnecessary work, this could be a serious and grave violation. Specifically, it seems this form of violation, in order to be serious, would require that the work be 1) truly unnecessary; 2) for selfish reasons; 3) be excessive.

This would also include those who impose this burden on others. For example, if a business owner sees an opportunity to make extra money by forcing employees to work on Sunday from 7 am – 7 pm even though those employees will be hindered from worship, family time and rest, this could be grave.

Full Knowledge: It's conceivable that there are many who do not fully understand the requirements of this Commandment. As a result, the cultural norms that seem to disregard the importance of the Lord's Day can cloud their thinking. For example, if someone grew up in a family that went to Sunday Mass only 90% of the time and, as a result, never truly understood that the requirement of attending Mass 100% was essential to God's will, they may not be fully responsible for missing. As always, this does not make it OK to miss Sunday Mass even once or twice a year. But it may mean that, if they do miss for what they rationalize as a "good reason," they may not be fully guilty of mortal sin. As with the other Commandments, God knows the heart and God knows the depth of knowledge and will judge accordingly.

Complete Consent of the Will: Let's say that you and your family were getting ready for Sunday Mass and you went to start the car and the battery was dead. You tried to get it started to no success. By the time you get it started you've missed the last Mass. Are you a sinner? Obviously not. You did miss your Sunday duty, but God sees clearly that this was not willful and will most certainly offer His grace to you and your family anyway.

There are other ways that someone could be partially responsible but not fully responsible for missing Mass or for committing other violations of this Commandment. For example, say a parent flew out for the weekend to visit an adult child in a different state. And say that this child no longer attends Mass. The parent asks to be taken to Mass and this adult child gets very upset and doesn't want to help. If that parent just gives into the pressure so as to "keep the peace," this is still the wrong choice but the emotional strain may actually reduce the personal responsibility of missing Mass that weekend. But with that said, it's important to note that the good witness of doing all one can to fulfill their Sunday duty is essential. Sometimes this will cause tension but we must remember that God's will must take precedence over everyone else. This is hard when the conflict is within the family, but we must make fidelity to God our primary goal no matter what the consequences.

4

LOVING YOUR FAMILY

The Fourth Commandment:

Honor your father and your mother, that you may have a long life in the land the LORD your God is giving you. (Ex 20:12)

For a summary of this commandment, read the *Catechism* #2199.

The first three Commandments are all about direct love and worship of God. In them we learn how to love God with our whole heart, mind, soul and strength. Commandments Four through Ten call us to love our neighbor as we love ourselves (Mark 12:31).

The Fourth Commandment especially highlights the natural and Christian understanding of the family. It focuses in on the responsibility that children have toward their parents, but it also gives insight into the role and duty of parents, spouses, all family relationships and civil authority. This Commandment covers a wide array of moral questions within the family and society as a whole. Therefore, rather than just looking at the bottom line and upper limit of this Commandment, let's look at it from various perspectives so as to get a more complete picture of all that the Fourth Commandment calls us to.

God's Plan for Parents

We begin our reflection on this Commandment by looking at it from the natural design of God. "God created mankind in his image; in the image of God he created them; male and female he created them. God blessed them and God said to them: Be fertile and multiply" (Genesis 1:27-28).

The most basic foundation of all society is marriage and the family. Male and female are called to come together and enter into a covenant of love. This love is a participation in God's life in the Trinity. The unity of husband and wife, established by the covenant they make through their vows, becomes the foundation for the begetting and raising of children.

Of course the ideal is not always achieved in life, but, nonetheless, the natural design of God for humanity is what we must see as the goal and foundation of human life. Family life, thus, becomes the most basic building block of all of society.

Ideally, it is the love of husband and wife that provides the proper context for children. The mutual love of spouses opens them to God's creative power to bring forth new life. And this mutual love that they share becomes the foundation for children to be raised in a healthy environment of love and unwavering commitment.

The duty of parents flows from their indissoluble and unconditional commitment toward each other. That love then overflows from their marriage to their children. This overflowing love is a reflection of the love of the Trinity in that the love of Father and Son is the Person of the Holy Spirit and the love of the entire Trinity overflows upon all of humanity.

The love of parents is such that they have certain duties and obligations toward their children. These duties also should be seen as certain privileges they have in begetting and raising their children.

The responsibilities (and privileges) that parents have begin with providing for their children's basic needs. They must feed them, clothe them, provide shelter and the like. Their duties, however, extend far beyond the basics. They are also called to nurture them emotionally, spiritually and intellectually. Parents must care for and nurture the whole person, body, mind, soul and spirit.

Practically speaking, this takes on many forms. Of greatest importance is the spiritual nourishment a parent is called to offer a child. This means that, more than anyone else, parents are called to teach their child the ways of faith. They are to teach them prayers and pray with them. They are to bring them to church and make sure they learn their catechism. They are to help them prepare for the reception of the sacraments so as to grow in grace. And they are to teach them how to live a moral life by their words and their actions. And they are to do all they can to nurture a deep, personal, intimate and loving relationship with our Triune God.

Closely connected to this essential duty and privilege is the importance of offering proper emotional and affective support and love. Humans need to give and receive love, and parents, more than anyone, must offer emotional, spiritual and human love to their children. This basic human need helps children to grow into balanced and healthy interpersonal beings who know, in turn, how to show proper love and affection toward others.

Being a Holy Child

The Fourth Commandment especially highlights the duty of children toward their parents. This certainly applies to young children, but it also applies to adult children. The sacred bond of parent and child may change over time, but it always remains. It's part of God's natural design for humanity and is also elevated to a supernatural level by His grace.

It's important to start this reflection by looking at the actual words of the Fourth Commandment carefully. It says, "honor" your father and mother. Note that it doesn't say, "obey" them. Of course, for children, obedience is part of the way they honor their parents. Let's look at how this is lived out in the family at all ages.

Authority of Parents: Parents are entrusted with a certain authority within the family. We begin by simply seeing it as a natural authority that is part of the design of God for human life. This authority encompasses many aspects of family life and is essential to the healthy unity and functioning of a family.

Authority can be abused. When that happens it causes a certain disruption in the good ordering of family life. Authority can also be neglected, and when that happens, disorder and a certain chaos are introduced. But when parental authority is lived in accord with God's plan, it brings unity, strength and stability to the family and helps children to grow into healthy and mature men and women.

Parental Obedience: One of the obvious responsibilities of parents is to exercise their proper authority over their children and to expect obedience from them. Children, in turn, honor the God-given authority of parents by submitting to their direction and honoring the authority they have over them. This is good when given and received properly! Of course it doesn't mean it's easy, but it is good.

Obedience is owed to a parent in all things that are in union with God's will. Obviously there are many moral requirements that parents must make of their children. These moral requirements help to form them into morally upright people.

On the flip side, if a parent were to act in an abusive way demanding a child act contrary to the will of God, the parent has no authority to do this and causes much damage. Children, for their part, are often left confused and hurt when this happens and, ideally, grandparents or other family members step in when it's blatant or abusive. But it's also true that no parent will be perfect and will inevitably make some mistakes that can more easily be overlooked and forgiven.

Obedience to parents includes numerous things. Parents should not hesitate to establish good "rules of the house" that are prudent and that are in the best interest of the healthy maturing of their children. Children need to learn self-discipline and responsibility in life and that often happens through the holy exercise of parental authority.

Honoring of Parents: Children, young and old, are all called to honor their parents, not only obey them. Though obedience is part of that "honoring" for young children, it's not the exclusive way they honor their parents. Children must also grow in respect for parents and learn to show that respect in their words and actions. Children learn to love others by first learning to love their parents. Parental love is the most important "training ground" for human love and for all healthy interpersonal and social interactions in the future. Therefore, the bond of love and honor between parent and child will have an enormous impact upon who they are and how they relate to people throughout their lives.

For that reason, parents should not hesitate to expect honor, in the proper sense, from their children. They should help to foster respect from their children by being parents who are worthy of respect. Of course all people deserve respect, but when a parent lives a truly honorable life filled with virtue and genuine goodness, this will help foster healthy honor and respect from their children. Therefore, one of the most important things a parent can do is to be a person that children truly look up to and admire as a result of their manifest virtue and goodness.

As children grow into young adulthood, their relationship with their parents will change. The obedience once owed to parents regarding normal daily living will not be necessary any longer nor will it even be helpful. Young adults, and subsequently adult children, need parents to expect them to slowly take more and more responsibility for their own lives. This is especially the case with all the minor things such as what time to go to bed, cleaning up after themselves, etc. It will also include more important things such as who their friends are, what jobs or careers they pursue, and the like. Though parents may always be called on at times to exercise a certain influence in the lives of their adult children, there must be a healthy balance so that adult children can take on responsibility in their lives and build on the foundation they were given by their parents throughout their childhood.

As adults, children will always be responsible to continue their love and respect for their parents. They must keep their parents as important parts of their lives, consult them and continually show love and respect toward them. This is much easier when a parent acts in the appropriate way toward their children. It is much more difficult when they are less "deserving" of that respect. It is especially difficult for adult children when their parents fail to respect them as adults and when a parent fails to properly "let go" of their children. This creates a tension that makes for a difficult relationship of proper honor.

Honoring of Elderly Parents: As the old phrase goes, "What comes around goes around!" In a sense, this is true with the parent/child relationship also. Parents are entrusted with the love and care of children as they grow. They must take care of their basic material needs as well as their emotional, psychological and spiritual needs.

But there will come a day for most parents when they can no longer take care of themselves properly due to their old age. When that happens, it is primarily the duty of adult children to care for their parents. This includes all the same needs mentioned above: material, emotional, psychological and spiritual. Yes, society as a whole has a certain responsibility toward the elderly such as healthcare, financial support (such as social security), etc. But the primary responsibility falls on adult children as a result of their duty to honor their parents.

Family Life

When parents are blessed with more than one child, their children also are blessed with the interaction of siblings. The natural intention of God for siblings is similar to that of parents minus the obedience part. Siblings offer each other the healthy opportunity to grow in mutual love and respect.

These family bonds offer a wonderful opportunity for children to learn many basic requirements of human relationships. For example, siblings are obliged to always work toward forgiveness of each other. While it's never good that siblings fight, it also seems to be inevitable. But God changes this into good in that He allows those moments of forgiveness and reconciliation within the family to be moments of mercy and healing. Siblings learn how to experience hurt from the sins of another and to then offer forgiveness and mercy. They also learn how to ask for forgiveness and how to receive it when they have hurt the others.

Siblings cannot disown each other in healthy families. Sure we've all heard stories of siblings who never speak to each other any longer. But especially in healthy families while growing up, it's not possible to ignore your sibling every day. And a good parent will help to foster reconciliation when needed. This offers a wonderful lesson for life. They learn, within the family, how to love, forgive and ask forgiveness. They learn what mercy is and what it means to have unconditional love. This is one of the natural blessings of family life as God intended it.

Affection within the Family: One basic human need is that of healthy and holy human affection. We were made to offer and receive proper affection for one another. When this becomes distorted, it can cause grave hurt and come out in destructive ways such as sexual abuse, anger, or resentment. But when lived well, proper family affection adds much to the healthy formation of children as they grow into healthy adults.

It's quite natural for a mother, for example, to coddle her newborn infant. And it's quite natural for that infant to cling to his/her mother. As a child grows that affection will change, but should always be there. A father's affection must also be present in the lives of his children and fulfills basic human needs. When offered appropriately, this affection helps to form a well-rounded young man or young woman.

The scope of this reflection does not include an in-depth analysis of the role of affection offered by father and mother. But it is worth pointing out that there are many studies that show the importance of both. Growing daughters and sons both have certain needs for the feminine love and affection of a mother and the masculine love and affection of a father. And there are many studies that reveal that those youth who lack one or the other, or receive it in a distorted way, are challenged in their affective maturity. That's not to say that God cannot bring help and healing, but it is important to acknowledge the importance of both a father's and a mother's love and affection.

Christian Family Life: Jesus came to Earth and entered into our human nature. He did this within the context of an earthly family. Jesus loved St. Joseph and His Blessed Mother as a child loves and was loved by them as parents love. He had cousins, aunts, uncles, grandparents, etc.

Ultimately, He sanctified human life by the sacrifice of His death and resurrection. And in sanctifying human life, He also sanctified family life. Thus, one of the effects of Jesus' life, death and resurrection was the institution of the Christian family.

The Christian family is distinguished from what we may call the "natural family" in the same way we distinguish our life of grace from our human nature. The Christian family is to be understood as a family in which Jesus' life, death and resurrection is alive and well. It means that this particular family is united not only by human natural bonds, but also by the grace of God.

A Christian family is one that prays together, speaks about faith and morality, practices charity and makes God the center of all they do. The

Christian family is also one that acts as a unique image of the love of the Trinity to the world. They "evangelize" by the witness of their love and unity in Christ. There are many levels of holiness each family may share in, just as there are many levels of holiness that individuals share in. Therefore, the closer each member grows toward perfection in Christ, the closer the entire family comes to reflecting the life of the Most Holy Trinity.

The Fourth Commandment and Society

The family is the most fundamental building block of all of society. This is a key point to understand! It's key so that the family is able to fulfill its role in society and it is also key to understand so that society and societal institutions do not infringe on the rights of any family.

As a building block of society, a society will ultimately be strong or weak not primarily because of the political system in place; rather, a society will be a reflection of the health of the families within it. If there are many strong families, society will be strong. If there is mass disunity and brokenness within many or most families, society will also begin to crumble.

The cultural and political leaders of any day and age must respect the institution of the family and not infringe upon it. Laws and cultural influences must largely strive to support the rights and the health of each family. Parents must be allowed to be parents and live their responsibilities out faithfully. Society must only intervene when there are clear abuses within a family.

Furthermore, an ideal society will foster laws and cultural influences that offer support to families as they strive to live out their sacred calling. When laws begin to conflict with these family rights, action must be taken.

The Role of Civil Authorities

In addition to respect for the family, the legitimate civil and societal authorities must be respected as a result of this Commandment. Here are a few ways this is fulfilled within society:

Law Enforcement: Within any society there must be laws. Laws are good when they help foster the good ordering of society and are in union with, or at least not opposed to, God's divine law. Therefore, this Commandment requires that we act in obedience to all civil laws that are legitimate.

Political and Civil Leaders: Just as within the family, obedience is not the only requirement of this Commandment. Respect and honor is also required. Therefore, this Commandment requires that we strive to show proper respect toward those within our community who have a unique role of governance. Even if we disagree with some political goal, we must respect the office of those in authority.

By extension, this Commandment calls us to honor anyone who serves the community. Those in the Military come to mind as people worthy of societal respect and honor.

Others in Authority: There are many others who hold a place of authority over us within society. For example, teachers must be obeyed and listened to as a result of this Commandment. Or, when we visit a private institution, such as a museum, we must show proper respect toward the rules of that museum and those in charge of it.

General Respect for All: Lastly, just as siblings must strive for mutual respect as a result of this Commandment, so also we must strive for respect for all people within society. We must care for the poor and needy, but we must also strive to show common courtesy toward anyone and everyone we meet.

A Summary of the Bottom Line and Upper Limit of the Fourth Commandment

The bottom line, as outlined above, is quite simple. This Commandment is broken when younger children fail to properly obey their parents. And parents break this Commandment when they abuse their rights toward their children. Adult children break this Commandment when they fail to properly care for their aging parents. And we all break this Commandment when we fail to show the proper respect for those in authority.

The upper limit of this Commandment is best achieved by striving for a deep love and respect for all people. Prayer, love, respect, honor, obedience and unity are the keys to healthy family life as well as life within the larger community. When we see others as images of God and as sacred, we will treat them with the dignity they deserve. We will do so not so much because we are trying to avoid sin; rather, we will do so because of the love God puts in our hearts for all people. We will be good and loving children, faithful parents, charitable siblings and excellent citizens. This Commandment calls us to foster true love and unity within our families first, but from there, within all of society.

Practical Considerations

As with the other Commandments, let's look at the ways that the Fourth Commandment is broken in a mortal way. From there, we will be able to see how it is also broken in venial ways.

Grave Matter: How is the Fourth Commandment broken in a grave way? The most extreme examples are as follows: Child abuse, serious disobedience toward parents, neglect or abuse of aging parents, complete disregard for civil laws and civil authority.

Since this Commandment especially highlights the responsibility of a child toward a parent, let's look at an example of this kind. Say, for example, a parent has clear rules for a teen that he must be in by 10 PM. The teen is in but at midnight sneaks out for a night on the town with a friend. This is a direct and serious violation of the Fourth Commandment. It's fair to say that this violation is also grave matter.

Full Knowledge: It's hard to conceive, in the example above, how this teen could not know that sneaking out at midnight is a violation of this Commandment. Perhaps one way this lack of full knowledge could happen is as follows. Say that this teen was never really given much of an explanation of the rules of the home and was at his friend's house talking with his friend's parents. The parents of his friend make a comment that there is nothing wrong with a teen going out in the middle of the night and that this teen's parents are too strict. They say that this is just "part of being a teenager!" After thinking about it, he decides that his friend's parents are right and that his parents are too strict. Therefore, he concludes that there is nothing wrong with just "being a teenager" and sneaking out at night.

Sneaking out is the wrong thing to do because it is a direct act of serious disobedience. But it is at least conceivable that this teen may not have fully understood that he ought not question the rules of his parents in this regard. If he rationalizes that his parents are too strict, he may lack the full knowledge due to the unhealthy influence of his friend's parents. As always, this does not make sneaking out OK, but it may reduce the personal guilt of this teen when he commits this grave violation of the Fourth Commandment.

Complete Consent of the Will: As with the other Commandments covered so far, it's clear that there are numerous pressures and influences on a teen. Say that a teen knows it is wrong to sneak out but every one of his friends sneak out on a regular basis. At school, that teen is teased continually being called a "mamma's boy" and "wimp." Finally, he caves in to the pressure so that others will stop teasing him. He knows it's wrong but is deeply struggling with the pressure of others. In the end, if he sneaks out, he did act in grave violation of this Commandment. But, as always, God knows the heart and the circumstances are such that he most likely was not 100% guilty in the eyes of God for his actions. If his guilt is diminished even slightly as a result of this extreme pressure and "bullying," he may not be fully guilty of a mortal sin.

Venial Sin: Venial sins are committed against this Commandment all the time within the family. No family is perfect so there will always be room for growth. Some venial sins in this area will be more serious, but many others will simply be a small lacking of the proper love, honor and respect we owe each other, especially those within our own family.

5

MURDER, ANGER AND HUMAN DIGNITY

The Fifth Commandment:

You shall not kill. (Ex 20:13)

You have heard that it was said to your ancestors, "You shall not kill; and whoever kills will be liable to judgment." But I say to you, whoever is angry with his brother will be liable to judgment (Mt 5:21-22)

If you were to watch the nightly news on any TV network or browse through the local newspaper there is a good chance you would come across the most recent story of murder. What a sad reality! Murder is horrific and of the greatest human tragedies. Perhaps, for that reason, it is also one of the most attention-grabbing headlines that can be reported.

Even in the Bible, one of the first stories we read is that of Cain killing Abel (Genesis 4:8). Murder has been around since the beginning of time and will forever remain one of the most shocking and awful actions within our world.

But is murder the only thing the Fifth Commandment speaks to us about? Certainly not. Murder, which is the intentional taking of innocent life, is perhaps the most serious way that this Commandment is violated. But working down from this ultimate destruction are many other forms of hate, anger and a lack of respect for the sacredness of human life.

Let's start with the bottom line ways that this Commandment is violated. From there, we'll look at ways that killing may actually be legitimate and a duty. We will conclude by looking at the ways that this

Commandment calls us to seek peace and respect the dignity of each person.

Bottom Line: Do Not Murder

The most direct violation of this Commandment is intentional murder. Within the umbrella of this offense are various factors and conditions to be explored. Additionally, there are sins and grave evils of omission and neglect that lead to the death or harm of others. These, too, are violations of this Commandment. Below is a summary of the primary ways that this Commandment is directly and indirectly violated.

Intentional Homicide: When one directly, willfully and intentionally takes the life of one who is innocent this is the gravest of sins. It is spoken of as a sin that "cries out to Heaven for vengeance." There is no justification for this and causes incredible harm. Among these grave sins, the gravest would be the killing of those within the family because this also violates a natural bond that must be respected. But any form of murder is grave and seriously flawed.

Abortion: Human life begins at conception. This is a fundamental truth that we must accept. It makes sense on a purely rational level and also makes sense on a scientific level. At the moment of conception the DNA of that new life is unique. This is human life. Therefore, we must accept the fact that, from the moment of conception, that new human life has the same dignity and rights as any human being.

One common distortion of the modern world is that the newly formed human being within the womb is somehow only part of the mother's body. Sure, the child cannot live separately from the mother's body. This is the way God designed the bringing forth of new life. But just because the new child cannot live on its own doesn't mean that it is any less sacred and deserving of any less respect and protection. Every life must be protected and cared for to the same degree.

Sometimes we hear it said, especially by politicians, that they support abortion only in cases of rape and incest. There is no doubt that these are horrific acts and the act of rape and incest must always and everywhere be condemned. Those who commit these acts must be held accountable and society must be protected from them so that they do not do this again.

With that said, it doesn't change the fact that new human life is new human life. Even if this new life came about through the tragic event of rape or incest, it is still human life. In this case, the extended family and all of society MUST strive to offer every bit of emotional, spiritual and even financial support necessary to help the mother bring that new life to birth. And after birth, everything must be done to help the mother make the right decision as to how this child will be raised either by her, her family or through adoption.

There is also the consideration of the mother's health. In rare cases there are tubal pregnancies. These are pregnancies that, according to current medical science, have a zero percent chance of success. In this case, and in this case alone, there is a traditional principle applied called "the principle of double effect." Double effect means that the doctor is permitted to remove the part of the fallopian tube that will soon rupture so as to save the mother's life even though he knows that this means the immediate death of the child. However, in this case, the intention is not abortion and, therefore, the death of the child is not intended. Rather, the death of the child is known but there is no other option and therefore is permissible. Additionally, if there is any way for the doctor to help the child attached to the fallopian tube to, instead, become attached to the uterus, this must be done. If it's not medically possible, then the removal of the part of the fallopian tube is the only option. Again, the death of the child is not intended directly in this case, it is only an unintended sad and unavoidable consequence.

There are also many other health concerns that can arise from pregnancy. In these cases every care must be taken to help the mother and child, but it is always wrong to intentionally and directly take the life of the child to help safeguard the mother's health. This is very difficult so, again, every care must be taken to help both mother and child to live and be healthy.

One sad practice as of recent is selective abortion. This happens when parents seek to find out if the child is healthy and find some form of genetic or other serious defect. Many times doctors will recommend abortion in the case of a child with clear physical "defects." This is never justified. It may be OK to have reasonable tests of this sort if the intention is to prepare the parents for any health concerns. But intentional abortion of a child with defects of any sort is still abortion and, thus, the murder of a disabled child.

Indirect Homicide: Related to intentional homicide would be a sin which brings about the death of another as a result of negligence of one's duty. Neglect, for example, by a parent toward a child which results in that child's death should be considered the most grievous of sins in this category.

Neglect could also happen by those with civil authority who fail to care for the needs of the people they are entrusted with. For example, if there is great poverty and hunger in a given society and the civil authorities have the ability to help rectify this but fail to out of selfish motivation, this is serious neglect and is sinful.

To a lesser extent, we are all, to a certain degree, to be considered our "brother's keeper." This means we are all called to be concerned for the good of others. If we neglect our duty to help the common good of others, we are partly responsible for the problems we could help solve. This may not only be neglect that results in the death of others, it may also include neglect that leaves others in poverty, despair, loneliness, and hurt. This could take on many forms so for our purposes we will stick to the general principles and let those principles be applied more directly in each particular circumstance of your life. Think about what you may have a duty to do to assist with the care and well-being of others, especially those with the greatest of needs.

Suicide: Suicide is the intentional taking of your own life. This is a topic that needs to be addressed directly, but also with a tremendous amount of nuance and care. First, suicide is always wrong. God is the author of life and only He has the right to take our life. We do not have complete rights over whether we live or die.

With that said, we should also be very careful to identify the many other questions that surround the choice of a person to take their life. Very often, when someone commits suicide the family is left in deep pain, confusion and loss. Many will wonder, "Is my child, spouse, friend, etc., in Hell now? Did they commit a mortal sin and, therefore, are they in Hell?" This is never a good question to even consider. The proper answer to that question is simply – don't go there!

Here is the reasoning for avoiding even that question. Yes, it's true, that the taking of our own life is grave matter. It is seriously wrong. However, it's very honest to follow that up by saying that it would be highly unlikely, and perhaps impossible, for a person to commit the act of suicide with full knowledge and complete consent of the will. Why? Because it is almost certain that a person who commits suicide is suffering from some sort of serious hurt, depression, confusion or the like. There is almost always some seriously diminishing circumstance that leaves the person with much less than full guilt for this action.

Suicide leaves deep wounds and many questions. The loved ones left behind will most likely wonder if they did something wrong, if they could have done something more, or whether they should have seen this coming. These are the "would haves, should haves, could haves." Family members should take great care to never fall into the deep regret that they "should have" done this or that.

Sure, over time the loss of a loved one may help you become more concerned and compassionate for others, especially other family members who are hurting. But dwelling on regrets and things that can no longer be changed will not bring your loved one back. Keep seeking to offer it to God and let God sort it out. God loves the one who committed suicide far more than anyone else and this all-loving and all-merciful God will do the right thing.

Euthanasia: One form of suicide that merits special attention is Euthanasia. Euthanasia is considered by many as "mercy killing." But, truth be told, there is nothing merciful about it. Sure, when someone is suffering gravely there is a tendency to want to relieve their suffering. In some cases, people will conclude that the suffering is bad enough to take their life so that the suffering will end. But this is a false sense of compassion at work.

The ideal, when someone is suffering, is to offer compassion to the extent needed. The actual word "compassion" means to "suffer with." It means that humans enter deeply into the lives of others and are there with them in their suffering. It means they love them in their suffering and help them to carry the heavy burden they are carrying.

True mercy is love for those who are in dire need of love in the way they need love. Taking their life may be the quickest and easiest way out of suffering, but it's not the most compassionate way to treat them. True compassion means we do all we can to help them live a dignified life, even in the midst of the greatest of suffering. We must help them find meaning even in their suffering and learn to unite that suffering to the Cross of Christ. Jesus knows pain and suffering. He lived it, identifies with it and can transform it. True compassion seeks to help the person offer their sufferings to Christ so that it is Jesus who takes those sufferings to His own Cross and produces the necessary peace a person needs to continue a life of dignity and strength.

Therefore, the direct killing of life, even if the person wants to die, is always wrong. God is the author of life and only God can take it. We never have a right to take our own life or to ask another to assist us with our own death, even if it appears to be the way out of some sort of suffering.

Lastly, it should be noted that when someone is at the end of their life, it may be of great benefit for them to receive pain medication. Sometimes pain medication will hasten the person's death. Here the principle of double effect also applies. In this case, if pain medication is given to alleviate present suffering, it is permissible as long as the intention is simply to alleviate the pain. This is permissible, and perhaps good to do, even if the unintended consequence is that the person dies more quickly. But this can become a slippery slope and great care must be taken. The medical professionals must be certain that the amount of pain medication given is not given in excess <u>so that</u> death will occur more quickly. This happens all too often and regular checks and balances must be in place so that pain medication is given only to a reasonable degree.

This is sufficient for our consideration of euthanasia. However, later in this chapter more will be said of other related questions regarding "end of life" issues and considerations.

Other Considerations: Furthermore, harsh speech, slander, ridicule, gossip and the like violate this Commandment because they "kill" another's character and good name. This violates their basic human dignity. Even thoughts of anger can be an interior violation of this Commandment. We are called to love and forgive and when we withhold love and forgiveness we break this Commandment.

Other violations would be the use of illegal drugs or abuse of prescription drugs, neglect of proper care of one's body, eating too much, sleeping too much, drinking alcoholic beverages in excess, being too concerned about one's health or appearance, racism, cruelty to animals and the like.

Human Dignity Must Be Respected

Respect for the salvation of others: We all have a duty to help foster the good of others. We must help them, by our words and example, to do good and avoid evil. When someone causes another to sin, this is scandal. Scandal is defined in the *Catechism* in this way: "Scandal is an attitude or behavior which leads another to do evil. The person who gives scandal becomes his neighbor's tempter" (#2284).

On the flip side, we should see in this Commandment a call to build up others and to help encourage them on the path of holiness. The goal is to be a witness to the good in our words and actions.

Respect for health and body: Our bodies are temples of the Holy Spirit and are to be cared for in that light. Therefore, abuse of our bodies through the excessive use of food or drink, alcohol or drugs is a violation of this Commandment. The goal is to take good care of our own health and to help foster the good health of others.

Science is a great blessing in that it unlocks the mysteries of the world as it was designed and created by God. But science has its moral limits. Specific examples of this are explained in the "Medical Ethics" section later in this chapter.

Torture can come under this heading in that it has to do with the direct harming of the body or mind for the purpose of eliciting information. This is contrary to the dignity of the human person and ought not be condoned even if it is judged that it will be effective in gaining important information. The dignity of the person, even those who are criminals, must always be respected.

Lastly, the direct mutilation of body parts is never permissible unless it is done for medicinal purposes such as amputation for the reason of stopping an infection.

Respect for the dead: Those who pass from this world are no longer dwelling in their bodies. However, the body is still sacred in that it was created by God and it will be raised up on the last day. Therefore, care should be taken to properly bury our loved one's remains so as to profess our belief in the resurrection of the body.

When Killing is not Murder

Is there a distinction between killing and murdering? Yes, there is. And it's an important one. The Fifth Commandment does not forbid us from killing; rather, it forbids us from murdering.

Murder is the taking of an innocent life without a just cause. Of course that definition makes it clear that, in some cases, there is a justifiable cause to take a life. That would be killing, but not murder. Let's look at the difference and some examples.

Legitimate self-defense: Self-defense is a right, and even a duty, that we all have. Jesus' Second Commandment summing up the entire moral law states: "Love your neighbor as you love <u>yourself</u>." Loving oneself certainly means we must defend ourselves and protect ourselves against the unjust aggression of others. Therefore, if someone is trying to do us grave harm, the right of self-defense is absolute.

However, we must make an important nuance in the right to self-defense and self-preservation. Say someone is angry with you and punches you, but in no way intends to seriously hurt you. Do you have a right to shoot them then and there? No, that would be doing more than was necessary to protect yourself. The right of self-defense permits you to do <u>only</u> that which is necessary to protect yourself. However, there are many rare but conceivable circumstances when your personal safety and defense ends with the need to deal your aggressor a lethal blow. In this case, it's important that your <u>intention</u> be that of self-defense as opposed to the intention of killing. There is a difference. Having only the intention of self-defense means you will do only that which is necessary to stop your aggressor. If the only good and reasonable option is something that may bring about the death of that person, it is permissible as long as they are coming at you with intent to kill you or do you serious harm. In this case, you intend self-defense but are aware of the secondary unintended possible effect of taking that person's life.

It's also important to note that some are called to protect the rights and the lives of others. For example, a parent has a duty to protect his/her child. If there is an unjust aggressor doing harm to one's child, the parent must intervene and, if the <u>reasonable</u> intervention results in unintended killing of the aggressor (meaning the intent was defense of the child), then that is permissible. The same is true of those entrusted with the protection of society such as police officers and the military. More will be said on this below.

Of course in these examples we are talking about very serious needs for self-defense. Very few people will ever experience such a need for this level of self-defense in their lives. But, nonetheless, it's important to understand this in principle even if the practical need is never made present.

Protection of society: There are those who have been entrusted with the protection of society. Domestically, police officers are on the front lines of the defense and safety of the community. Nationally, the military is entrusted with our defense. In both of these groups the principles above apply and killing is permitted when it is the only appropriate means of the protection of others.

For police officers (and the like), they have their responsibility given them by the just authority within a community. The local, State or Federal government will commission them to follow certain practices and procedures to keep the community safe. Sometimes those practices will involve the stopping of an unjust aggressor with lethal force. Good checks and balances should always be in place to make sure that excessive force is not exercised. But as long as the officer acts within his/her legitimate authority, it is, at times, not only their right but even their duty to use lethal force to protect the citizens whose care they are entrusted with.

The military is to follow the same principles of self-defense. It is just to go to war when the legitimate authority (the president, for example) declares war so as to stop the unjust aggression of a group or another country. There are two things to note here. First, the commander-in-chief must make the prudent judgment as to whether or not this is a just war. And, second, those in the military must act with lethal force only when necessary and only to stop those who are the aggressors when the legitimate authority (the commander-in-chief) has given permission. With that said, here are the basics of the morality behind the "Just War Theory."

Just War Theory: The following are the conditions set down by the *Catechism* (#2309) supporting a war as just:

—the damage inflicted by the aggressor on the nation or community of nations must be lasting, grave, and certain;

—all other means of putting an end to it must have been shown to be impractical or ineffective;

—there must be serious prospects of success;

—the use of arms must not produce evils and disorders graver than the evil to be eliminated. The power of modern means of destruction weighs very heavily in evaluating this condition.

Basically, going to war is only permitted when it is necessary to protect the nation from serious and continuous harm from an unjust aggressor, everything else has been tried to bring peace, war appears to be a legitimate way of ending the unjust aggression, and the end result is judged to be better than the current situation. These conditions must all be met before the commander-in-chief of any nation declares war.

What if these conditions are not met? Are those in the military still obliged to go to war? This enters into a grey area but, as a general rule, unless the dictates of the commander-in-chief are obviously immoral, those serving in the military should be comfortable following orders. The reason is that very often the details of war decisions are not known by the general population. There are many factors that are "top-secret" and available to the country's leaders alone. Therefore, when a commander-in-chief states that the war is just, it should be presumed just unless there is clear knowledge that it is not. And if it is clearly known that the war is unjust, those serving in the military must not follow the directions of the commander-in-chief. However, if this were to happen, those serving in the military should first turn to the Church and seek advice from the bishops on the morality of war in particular situations.

Capital Punishment: In some cases it is legitimate for the State to put people to death. But in our day and age this is rare. There is only one case in which capital punishment is acceptable. It is acceptable only when the State has judged that the criminal, guilty of a capital crime, is a grave threat to society and that the only means of safeguarding society is to put this person to death. However, be careful in this consideration. The fact is that, in our day and age, most countries are perfectly capable of having reasonable certainty that a dangerous criminal can be incarcerated for the rest of his life and, thus, society can be kept safe without the need for putting this person to death.

The key here is that the State need not have *absolute* certainty the person will never escape - that level of certainty would be impossible. The principle at work here is the reasonable protection of society while at the same time recognizing the dignity of the person who committed a heinous crime. The hope is his conversion and repentance.

With that said, it is conceivable that there are some cultures in which the permanent incarceration of a criminal is not all that possible. In that case, if it is an honest and reasonable judgment of the State that the death penalty is the only way to protect society from this criminal, it could be permissible.

In this case it is not murder in that it is not the taking of <u>innocent</u> life and it is done by the legitimate authority.

Other "Medical Ethics" Considerations

One major area of modern moral decisions is that of medical ethics. At the time of Jesus, medicine was obviously not what it is today. For that reason, modern science has raised many new questions for consideration. Below are various issues that deserve special attention. However, this listing is by no means comprehensive. Therefore, understanding the general moral principles are key to being able to make good moral decisions in all specific questions that arise in modern medicine.

In vitro Fertilization: In vitro fertilization (IVF) is the scientific process of removing eggs from a woman and artificially fertilizing them with the sperm of a man. Once fertilization takes place in a lab setting, the fertilized eggs are then inserted into the womb of the woman in the hopes that at least one of them will implant on the uterine wall and pregnancy will occur. This process is immoral for two basic reasons.

First, even though conception is possible in this artificial environment, it is contrary to the laws of nature that God established for the begetting of children. There are many couples who deeply desire to have children and are not able to do so. This can cause a deep sorrow and lead couples to look into other options. In this case, it's important to note that just because a scientific procedure may work, it is not, therefore, automatically morally permissible to use. IVF is akin to taking the act of creation into our own hands. God is the author of life and offered a natural way for that to happen. If this natural way does not produce pregnancy there are morally licit ways of assisting pregnancy such as fertility medication and Natural Family Planning. IVF separates the natural design of the begetting of children from pregnancy. It separates pregnancy from the sexual act of husband and wife and for this reason the Church has discerned it is a practice that is contrary to the natural plan of God and ought not be used.

Secondly, IVF brings with it the grave danger of the loss of human life. Most often, several eggs are fertilized and implanted with the knowledge that some or most of these new beginnings of human life will not live. Therefore, using this method disregards the sacredness of every human life at the moment of conception by bringing forth human life that has a poor chance of survival. This goes at the heart of the question of when life begins. Since life begins at conception as the Church teaches and science affirms, it is irresponsible and gravely illicit to create human life in a seriously hazardous condition in the hopes that at least one of those new embryos will live.

With that said, if a child is conceived and implanted using this method, and this child grows to maturity and is born, it's important to know that this child is no less sacred and has no less dignity given the way it was conceived. Life is life and it is all sacred and precious. The end does not justify the means, but, nonetheless, when the "end" is a child, it is sacred and is to be treated with the greatest dignity.

Cloning: The attempt to clone a human being is always immoral. The reason is very similar to the first point mentioned above in IVF.

Cloning undermines the natural design of God for bringing forth new life and, therefore, is contrary to nature and is contrary to human dignity.

Again, just because science may have the ability to do something doesn't mean it is right in doing it. In this case, experiments with human cloning are gravely immoral and should never be attempted.

Organ transplant: Jesus said, "No one has greater love than this, to lay down one's life for one's friends" (John 15:13). This high calling can be realized in many ways. One way is to allow for the legitimate donation of organs for the life and health of another.

Certainly, if donating an organ would bring about the direct death of a person this is immoral since it is the taking of an innocent life. But, when someone has died, or has been declared "brain dead," it is permissible to use their organs for the good of others.

With that said, it's important to have medical certainty of brain death prior to the harvesting of organs. This would be a medical decision based on a reasonable and certain conclusion that if a person were taken off of life support, they would immediately die. And that's the key. This can get into a certain grey area and great care must be taken since most organs must be "harvested" while the heart is still pumping while on artificial life-support. Only when a determination of brain death is made is it morally licit to move forward while the person is still on life support. In this case, it is understood that only the body is living but the person is actually dead.

Other "End of Life" Decisions

The end of life will come to us all. And most will enter into certain moral decisions regarding the end of their loved one's life. In order to make good moral decisions regarding end of life decisions and what sort of care and treatment is to be given or can be avoided, it's important to know the basic language.

Care vs. Treatment: First, it's important to note a difference between "care" and "treatment." Care must always be given. This is a requirement of basic human dignity. What is care? Care includes all the basic human needs such as food, water, love, comfort, and basic medicines. Treatment would encompass all forms of medical procedures or medications that are more invasive.

Ordinary vs. Extraordinary Means: One very important key distinction to understand when making moral decisions of a medical nature is that of ordinary and extraordinary. Ordinary care is always required and includes all the basic needs we must meet as a result of our human dignity. Nutrition and hydration, for example, most always fall under this heading (more on that to follow). Ordinary care would also include basic hygiene, emotional and spiritual support, comfort care and any medical procedures or medications that are not too burdensome.

Extraordinary care and treatment would include most medical procedures that in some way impose a burden on the person. The key is that the treatment itself is a burden. In many cases it would be morally necessary to provide extraordinary care, but in some cases extraordinary care can be denied. A few examples will help explain.

Say a person is in stage four cancer and will certainly die. There is an option of using heavy doses of chemotherapy to slow the progress down but that will most likely cause the person to be quite sick and will, therefore, impose a heavy burden on the person. Say that this person is 95 years old and is mentally and spiritually ready to meet Jesus. In this case it is understandable if the person rejects the invasive and burdensome extraordinary treatment of chemotherapy so as to allow nature to take its course.

On the other hand, say there is a 35 year old person who has several small children. They discover cancer early and the chemotherapy recommended may have a decent chance of working. The doctors explain that the treatments will be very burdensome and cause serious illness, but it's the best option. In this case, the extraordinary care should be chosen.

The main determining factor is to decide whether or not the actual treatment itself imposes too much of a burden on the person. By burden we may mean a physical, psychological or even financial burden. In other words, is the treatment simply too much to ask? If the best prudential judgment is that the treatment is too much and imposes too much of a burden then it can be declined.

Another factor to consider is that of medical success. If the treatment given has little to no chance of success and is judged futile by the doctor, this should be seriously considered in making a final judgment. A futile treatment that imposes a serious burden can be declined.

On the other hand, extraordinary means do not necessarily need to be declined. If a person is up to it and is desirous of the treatment and believes the benefit outweighs the burden then it is OK to seek it out.
In determining whether or not something is too burdensome there is an important distinction that must be made. Sometimes, the erroneous judgment is made that <u>my life itself</u> is too burdensome and, therefore, various treatments are denied so as to expedite death. This is a problem because we should never make what we call "quality of life decisions." In other words, it is not proper to say that my "quality of life" is so poor that I will deny even ordinary treatments so as to alleviate my suffering or the possible "imposition" my life may be on my loved ones.

The distinction to make is whether or not the <u>treatment</u> proposed is too burdensome. This is different than saying <u>my life</u> is too burdensome. For example, say a person has a serious illness that causes much pain. There is a medical treatment (such as a medicine) that can be given and that treatment imposes little to no burden. Is it permissible to deny the treatment because the person wants to die and alleviate their suffering? No, this would not be proper. In this case the goal is to give the non-burdensome treatment AND to do all that is possible to help the person with their suffering. Emotional, psychological, spiritual and physical care must be given to help the person who is suffering. But denying basic treatment that imposes little to no burden is a form of euthanasia by neglect. The only time that ordinary treatments of this sort may be denied are when they are judged futile (ineffective).

Nutrition and Hydration: One area that requires special attention is that of nutrition and hydration. Ordinary means of nutrition and hydration should always be given. This means that as long as the person is able to eat and drink, food and water should be given. It would be wrong to starve someone. The most common decision regarding food and nutrition that people struggle with involves <u>artificial</u> nutrition and hydration. This would be most often the insertion of a feeding tube.

Feeding tubes provide a way for a person to continue with the basic care they need when they are not able to eat or drink on their own. This is especially the case of someone in a permanent vegetative state. The clear teaching of the Church on this is that a feeding tube should be considered ordinary care unless one of two conditions is met.

The first condition in which a feeding tube could be denied is that of futility. Futility means, for example, that the person is not able to receive nourishment from the food. This could happen if they have a serious form of stomach cancer which does not allow the food to be absorbed into the body. In this case, using a feeding tube will not help and, therefore, it is not necessary. In fact, it may even be harmful.

The second case in which a feeding tube could be denied is when the person is so weak or elderly that even the medical procedure of inserting a feeding tube is too burdensome. In this case, it is determined that the procedure is too much and, therefore, is permissible to decline. If, however, a feeding tube is already in place and the person does physically benefit from its nutrition, then the food should be given.

As described above, all "quality of life" decisions should be avoided. A person should not be denied food and hydration, even if given artificially, as a way of starving them so that death will come.

With all of the decisions above it is essential that a doctor be carefully consulted so that the medical facts are determined. Is it a futile treatment? How burdensome is the treatment? What are the chances of success? After these facts are known, it is then left to the best judgment of loved ones to make a good decision based on the moral principles of medical ethics described above.

The Upper Limit

Respect: The ultimate goal we are called to in this Commandment is that of respect for the human person. We must respect all life from the moment of conception until the moment of natural death. Respect for life means we see the innate dignity of everyone. We care for the unborn, the marginalized, the poor, the hungry, the elderly and the sick. We respect and love our family, neighbor and all people as images of God.

Seeking peace: The upper limit for a community or nation is to seek peace. This means first and foremost freedom from armed conflict and oppression of people. But it also means creating an environment and society which fosters opportunities for the mutual well-being of all its citizens. Charitable organizations must be encouraged and supported nationwide and even across national lines so as to bring about not only an end to conflict, but also a culture of love and unity.

Practical Considerations

Let's now look at the three conditions of mortal sin as it applies to the Fifth Commandment:

Grave Matter: As outlined above, there are numerous ways that this Commandment is broken in a grave way. Any direct and intentional killing of the innocent is grave. Furthermore, serious acts of violence, anger, or neglect are grave actions or omissions.

Full Knowledge: Murder, serious violence or serious neglect are known by most everyone to be gravely wrong. We just know that we ought not do damage to another. One example of how one may not have full knowledge was explained in Chapter One under the heading of "Erroneous Conscience." Rather than repeat this example here you may want to go back to that section for a reminder.

Complete Consent of the Will: This factor of a mortal sin is, perhaps, most easily understood as a more likely diminishing factor of guilt. Very often, when violence is enacted, it is done in a moment of rage and extreme emotion. This is no justification since we have a duty to have our emotions and passions under control. However, one can conceive of a sudden shocking situation in which a person acted in a seriously harmful way without really thinking about it.

Say, for example, that someone comes home to find a spouse in the act of adultery. This is shocking and evokes extreme emotion. Say that the shocked spouse reacts with sudden anger without any premeditation. In that sudden act of anger the adulterer is killed.

Obviously this is a very sad situation and killing, in this case, is not justified. However, that intense emotion may mean that the person's sin does not rise to the level of being mortal sin. Even the civil laws of most countries recognize a difference between premeditated murder and "temporary insanity."

Furthermore, any grave factors, especially of an emotional form, can have the effect of lessening the personal guilt of one who gravely violates this Commandment. As always, that does not make the action good or even neutral, it only lessens the personal guilt.

Venial Sins: The Fifth Commandment can be violated in numerous venial ways. Words, for example, when harsh, belittling, condescending or sarcastic can "kill" another's spirit. Verbal abuse does much damage to others, especially when done within the family.

All forms of anger, passive aggression, or mean-spirited actions violate this Commandment. We must strive to love and respect the whole person, body, mind and spirit. When one is harmed mentally, spiritually or physically, this Commandment is broken. Of course, verbal, emotional and spiritual abuse can also rise to the level of grave matter, but very often it remains as a less serious venial sin.

Envy is also a violation of this Commandment. Envy is distinguished from jealousy in that jealousy is more of a covetousness and unhealthy desire to have what others have. This could be jealousy of their possessions, personal qualities, social status or the like. Envy often begins with a certain jealousy but adds to it some form of harmful acting out toward the other. Envy is a deep sorrow over the good of others and leads one to try and damage them as a result. Anger is always involved in envy but is often internal, causing the aggression to be more passive and subtle.

Finally, this Commandment is broken even when we act in a negligent way and fail to properly build up others. We have a duty to love and support others. When we fail to do so we are partly responsible for the ill effects this has on them. Thus, it is possible to damage another by neglecting them and neglecting the love we owe them.

6

CHASTITY, PURITY, AFFECTION
AND MARITAL LOVE

The Sixth Commandment:

You shall not commit adultery. (Ex 20:14)

You have heard that it was said, "You shall not commit adultery." But I say to you, everyone who looks at a woman with lust has already committed adultery with her in his heart. (Mt 5:27-28)

Sexuality. Is that a "dirty" word? Certainly not. The Sixth Commandment presents to us the natural and supernatural design of God for human sexuality. Sexuality is intrinsic (meaning natural) to humanity and is inseparable from who we are. Discovering and understanding God's plan for sexuality as a whole will help us live out our sexuality in our lives.

We are Sexual Beings

It is not possible to separate sexuality from being human. We were created with affections, desires and the ability to love. These desires are good and holy but can also become distorted and sinful.

Love of neighbor is lived and expressed in many ways. As human beings we love not only with a spiritual love, but also with human affection. Our sexuality is ultimately one concrete and very human way of expressing and giving love.

Sexual love takes on various forms depending on who it is we are loving. Though we may not normally speak in these terms, it's accurate to say that our love is expressed through our sexuality to everyone we offer love. Parents to children, friend to friend, husband to wife and neighbor to neighbor, love is expressed through our human sexuality.

Often times when we speak of "sexuality" we mean only one form of sexual love – that shared between husband and wife through the marital act. But sexuality must be seen in a much broader context if understood properly and completely.

Let's start with Jesus. Did Jesus express sexual love? Well, yes. Of course we must be very careful to nuance this properly so we do not slip into some sort of heresy! Jesus was a human and was a man. Therefore, he loved as a human and as a man. He expressed His divine love through His human and masculine heart to all whom He encountered.

Loving as a man or as a woman, through our masculinity or femininity, is normal and healthy. Only when that human love becomes distorted and the other becomes an object of one's disordered desires is sin involved.

With that said, it would also be wrong to withhold human love from those we are called to love. This often happens when there is an inability to love in a healthy, human and affectionate way in accord with God's plan and in accord with the virtue of chastity. When a person's affections and sexual desires are disordered they not only tend to see others as objects in a selfish way, they are also often unable to show good and healthy affection and human love as a man or woman should.

God made us male and female. This complimentarity of the sexes must be appreciated, understood and properly lived. A mother will show affection for her child differently than a father will. Two female friends will relate to each other differently than two male friends. And spouses will strive to love and respect each other as the completion of who they are through a total gift of self, including a total gift of sexual love. The two shall be made one! And this unity is made possible in large part by the natural design of the complimentarity of the sexes.

The Upper Limit: God's Plan for Sexuality

The Universal Virtue of Chastity: In order to love in a healthy and holy way, the virtue of chastity is essential. This virtue is not only something for those who are single. It's a virtue that is essential to all people, including spouses.

Chastity means that a person surrenders his or her sexual passions to the will and design of God. It means that one's sexual desires are ordered to the good of another and expressed properly within each relationship.

True chastity frees a person to love and express that love in a human way without objectifying the other. Chastity means that one's human sexual passions are not selfish; rather, they become selfless, seeking the good of the other and expressing the love of God to others through their human hearts.

Temperance is an essential help to chastity. Temperance is all about self-control. It's also about "God-control" in the sense that it ultimately requires grace from God to become fully in control of one's passions. Temperance enables one to refrain from unhealthy desires that are contrary to the will of God, contrary to human dignity and contrary to one's vocation.

But chastity goes beyond temperance also. Chastity is not just about being in control of excessive and disordered sexual passions. Chastity also draws a person to the heights of human love and the ability to live and express that love in a holy way. It begins with self-control and ends with God living in and transforming our human nature into an instrument of His love of others.

Love of Husband and Wife: Among the many unique forms of human love is the love of husband and wife. This love is unique in that there is exclusivity, permanence, and fruitfulness at the heart of this love. This love, made holy by a sacred covenant before God, is invited to share in the exclusive giving and receiving of the body in accord with the natural design of God. Thus, the "sexual act" is a unique way through which human sexuality is expressed within the covenant of marriage.

Sexual love, within marriage, invites spouses to a self-gift expressed in physical intercourse. Though this act can become lustful and distorted even within marriage, it is ideally a unique way of expressing the unconditional and total gift of self which is central to the marriage covenant.

Sexual love within marriage must be total and fruitful. Therefore, the marital act is one of the most unique and sacred human expressions of love God gave us. The marital act is reserved solely for the covenant of marriage by its very nature in that it seals and renews the marriage covenant of a total and permanent gift. It also must, by its very nature, be open to the possibility of new life in accord with the natural design of God.

The Bottom Line: Abuses of Sexual Love

There are many ways that sexuality is abused. The principles and ideals above should be the measure for all sexual activity and affection. When sexuality fails to live up to these ideals, sin is committed. Below are some specific examples of how sexuality is abused and, therefore, how the Sixth Commandment is broken.

Adultery: Adultery is the willful breaking of the marriage bond through one or both spouses by engaging in sexual intercourse with another. It is a full expression of lust since adultery cannot be an expression of authentic pure love. Sexual intercourse is intended by the design of God to be embraced exclusively within the context of the marriage covenant. Jesus took this further (as we will see in the next section on the Ninth Commandment) when he said, "everyone who looks at a woman with lust has already committed adultery with her in his heart" (Matthew 5:28). Adultery causes grave damage to marriage and family life and introduces disorder into society. Sexual intercourse is such a powerful act that it is not possible to maintain a strong marriage and commit adultery at the same time. Adultery, by necessity, does grave damage not only to the souls of those committing it, but also to the marriage being offended.

Fornication: Not every sexual act outside of marriage is referred to as "adultery" strictly speaking. When neither person is married the sin is properly called "fornication." Fornication could be a onetime act with someone who is not well known, or it could be a more habitual sin committed between persons who have a regular relationship. The bottom line is that the sexual act is for marriage. Sexual intercourse outside of this context is always a grave evil.

Free Union: A free union could be considered a sub-set of fornication. This would include the persons who have a loving relationship but are not yet married. They may be thinking of marriage but have not made the permanent commitment.

In this case, if they enter into sexual relations either once or on a regular basis they are living a lie. The sexual act is a way of sealing the marital covenant that has already been made. It's not to be used as a sort of "testing ground." You cannot test marriage and all that makes up marriage. When this is attempted the person is saying two contradictory things. First, by the act of sexual intercourse one says, "I give myself to you completely and faithfully forever and am open to new life." But the lack of a marital commitment says, "I'm not sure I'm totally and permanently committed and am not ready to raise children within this context God designed." Therefore, sex even between those who love each other is gravely sinful if outside the marriage covenant.

Divorce: The sad reality of divorce must be understood from various points of view. This is especially necessary so that those who have gone through a divorce can properly sort out what happened so as to bring healing to their lives.

First, it's proper to say that divorce is sad. People do not enter into marriage with the intention of one day getting divorced. No matter the reasons for a divorce it most likely is a very painful experience.

Let's start with a proper understanding of separation so that we can put divorce in perspective. The Code of Canon Law states this regarding legitimate separation of spouses:

> If either of the spouses causes grave mental or physical danger to the other spouse or to the offspring or otherwise renders common life too difficult, that spouse gives the other a legitimate cause for leaving, either by decree of the local ordinary or even on his or her own authority if there is danger in delay. (Canon 1153 §1)

What does this tell us? It tells us that the Church fully understands that, in some cases, it's better for spouses to separate. Separation is certainly different than divorce in that separation acknowledges that the marriage bond still exists. The intent here is to simply offer the context that, in some cases, it's better that married couples separate at least for a time. With that said, sometimes separation leads to civil divorce. Volume Two of this series, *My Catholic Worship!*, gives more details on marriage, divorce and annulments which will not be repeated here. Please see that book for more information.

Regardless of the circumstances and regardless of who is or is not at fault in a divorce, it must be said that divorce itself introduces hurt and disorder into people's lives as well as into society. It hurts the spouses, the children, extended families and many others. It's simply honest to state this fact without placing any blame or guilt. In fact, one spouse may be completely innocent of any wrongdoing and may have done all that he/she could to make the marriage work. But it takes two to make it work, so when one or both fail in their responsibilities it's important to honestly acknowledge that this is not the ideal and that it is painful. Of course God can do all things and can even bring hope, healing and blessings out of any painful situation. Therefore, when divorce does happen it's essential to seek the guidance of the Holy Spirit and to rely upon the Church for clarity and healing.

Divorce itself may or may not be a personal sin of the individual spouses. Most likely, one or the other has sinned in some way but it's very possible that the other has not.

Polygamy: Polygamy is the act of attempting a semblance of marriage between three or more people. Polygamy is a sin in two ways. First, it's a sin against the dignity of marriage in that it undermines the natural design of marriage being between one man and one woman. Polygamy is also a sexual sin when sexual relations take place. Marriage is the only proper context for sexual relations and marriage is only marriage when it takes place between one man and one woman. An attempt to enter into a different form of marriage is a sin against nature and when it involves sexual activity it is a sin against the Sixth Commandment.

Contraception: This is a very real and, for many, a very difficult part of the Sixth Commandment to consider. Methods of contraception today are very advanced and very prevalent. Perhaps in part for that reason, the Church teaching on contraception is ignored by many if not by most Catholics. Therefore, it is important to offer a clear and concise explanation so that this beautiful teaching will be embraced by all.

By "contraception" we mean the following: *Any intentional form of excluding or hindering the possibility of conception from the sexual act of married couples.* Read that definition a few times before you read on.

To understand why contraception is a sin it's important to reiterate the purpose of sexual intercourse. Sexual intercourse is an action that God gave to married couples to achieve two things: <u>unity</u> and <u>children</u>. First, unity takes place through sexual intercourse in that it is one natural way that couples express their love and renew their marriage covenant. It is a way of renewing their commitment of being a complete gift to the other. Therefore, intercourse is not just physical, it is also spiritual and emotional in that it solidifies and continues to fortify the marriage bond.

Secondly, sexual intercourse must always and everywhere be open to the possibility of new life. This is an <u>essential</u> part of the act of sexual intercourse. By "essential" we mean that God designed intercourse in such a way that if couples intentionally exclude the natural possibility of begetting children from any act of intercourse, they are sinning against the Sixth Commandment and against nature itself. This is hard to accept for many but it's true.

With that said, it is abundantly obvious that there are only a limited number of years and only certain times each month when a woman can get pregnant. Thus, it is also part of the natural design of God that most of the time intercourse takes place, conception will not happen.

Embracing this natural design of God is good and proper. In fact, if a couple discerns that it is best to avoid pregnancy at the time, they are encouraged to use methods of Natural Family Planning to scientifically discover when the woman is and is not fertile. Having sexual relations during the infertile periods and refraining during the fertile periods is permitted and, in some cases, may be best.

The main problem comes when something is done (contraception) to hinder the natural cycle of a woman or to interrupt the act of sexual intercourse so as to avoid pregnancy. This is a sin against nature itself and a sin against this Commandment because it intentionally excludes one of the <u>essential</u> parts of sexual intercourse, namely, openness to conception. Again, when the wife is past child bearing years or is not ovulating then God Himself has excluded the possibility of conception from that act of intercourse by His natural design. God is free to do this, we are not morally permitted to render the fertile periods infertile by our own will and actions.

Some medical/medicinal forms of contraception also add another problem in that they can have the effect of making implantation of the embryo difficult which is ultimately an early act of abortion. For this reason, some forms of contraception are worse than others.

The bottom line is that sexual relations should be embraced and lived in the way God designed it. It must always and everywhere fulfill the following: 1) Be only between spouses; 2) Have the intent of unity and the renewal of the marriage covenant; and 3) Be open to the natural design of God for the begetting of children without hindering that natural design.

Natural Family Planning (NFP), as mentioned above, is a legitimate way for spouses to be open to using the natural design of God regarding a woman's fertility. But it must also be said that even with NFP, there can be a danger not of contraception, but of a "contraceptive mentality." A contraceptive mentality is different than contraception in that it does not directly hinder the natural design of God for sexual intercourse. Instead, this is a mentality in which couples use NFP to an extreme and negligent way by deciding to avoid pregnancy for selfish reasons. For example, God may actually be saying to spouses, "I want to bless you with another child." And the couple fails to listen to this and, instead, decides that another child is not what they want. Therefore, they continually use NFP as a way of avoiding pregnancy. This is not a sin against the sexual act itself since they are using NFP. Instead, it's a sin against marriage and the will of God. This is tricky and requires honest discernment on the part of spouses. It's "tricky" in that there are times when God may very well be saying to a couple that it's His will they use NFP to avoid pregnancy at the time. This may be for serious emotional, mental, financial or other reasons. It may be that the couple is simply not ready to care for another child at that time. This is good to discern and, in this case, it is good to use NFP to avoid pregnancy. The key is to continually remain open to what God is saying and to continually strive to discern His will for their family.

Masturbation: Though masturbation is more common than many would like to admit, it is always a violation of this Commandment. It's important to state that up front. Masturbation is an abuse of the natural sexual desires. Sex is made for marriage and only marriage.

With that said, it's only honest to point out that many struggle with it. It's a struggle most likely for two reasons. First, because the sexual appetite is very powerful. Second, because masturbation is a very easy way to try and satisfy that powerful desire. It's important to point out that masturbation is only a way to "try" to satisfy that desire. Sure, many find a certain satisfaction in it since it causes many natural endorphins to be released and can cause a certain natural and physical satisfaction. But it never has the ability of truly satisfying and satiating the natural desires. Again, sex is made for marriage and only in marriage can it find its fulfillment.

Pornography: Pornography is an abuse of sexuality on many levels. First, it's what we call an "objectification" of the person being exposed. Even if that person freely consents to exposing him or herself, it's still an abuse of their innate beauty and dignity. In fact, in many ways we can say that what's wrong with pornography is that it shows too little rather than too much. In other words, it fails to reveal the true beauty and dignity of a person choosing, instead, to reveal only that which appeals to the carnal and disordered fleshly appetites.

Pornography is also abusive in that it does grave damage to the one looking at it. A person who looks at pornography stirs up many passions that are meant for marriage. In stirring them up in this disordered way, they allow their sexual passions to become even more disordered. This disordered "toying with" one's sexuality can become an addiction and can lead one into a habitual practice of trying to satiate these disordered desires. In fact, modern brain science has shown that an addiction to pornography is similar to an addiction to other drugs in that it releases many of the same chemicals in the brain that drugs do.

Prostitution: Prostitution is quite straight forward and it should be clear why this is a violation of this Commandment. It gravely violates the sacred dignity of the prostitute and does her/his soul much harm.

Rape: Again, it should be obvious why this is a horrible and grave violation of this Commandment and the dignity of the one being abused. One key to point out is that any sexual act should be done freely and lovingly between spouses. Rape not only objectifies a person, it also abuses them violently and offends the freedom they have. Therefore, it's not only a grave sexual abuse, it's also an abuse against the free will of the one abused and could be seen as a violation of the Fifth Commandment also: "Thou shall not kill."

Homosexual practices: This is a very sensitive topic in our day and age and, therefore, must be addressed with clarity and compassion. There are many things to consider with homosexuality and sexual activity between those of the same sex. Note the distinction between "homosexuality" and "sexual activity between those of the same sex." Having homosexual desires and tendencies is not a sin. Acting in a sexual way with another person of the same sex is a sin.

We begin with a short reminder that sexual intercourse is naturally designed by God to be used between a man and a woman after they have entered into the covenant of marriage. Homosexual marriage is contrary to the nature of male and female and contrary to the natural design of God for humanity.

This is becoming increasingly difficult for some to accept. Why? Perhaps because there are an increasing number of people who are starting to express the conviction that they <u>are</u> homosexual. This is a dangerous road to go down because by believing this (that I am homosexual) it causes a person to take their identity in their sexual desires. This is a very important point to understand. Sexual desires are most often quite unreliable as a guide to use to define one's life. When one says, "I <u>am</u> homosexual," they often mean that they have a desire to be with someone of the same sex either sexually or simply to fulfill a human need of love and companionship. This is often also translated into a justification for same-sex sexual activity.

But what we ought to take our identity in is that we are sons or daughters of God. Therefore, it's only proper to say, "I am a man and a son of God," or "I am a woman and a daughter of God." Our identity must be in who we are, not in what our sexual appetites are drawn to.

Regarding sexual appetites and desires, they are unreliable in that they are easily swayed and confused. But this brings up the question as to whether or not homosexual desires are natural or learned. Do they come from "nature" or from "nurture" as the question has often been phrased? This is a question that cannot be answered. Many will say they are simply born with these desires and, therefore, they should be able to act on them. This seems to be the growing belief of modern society. Others will say that homosexual desires come as a result of various social and personal conditions or as a result of various personal choices made in the past.

In answering this question we must strive to separate out a desire from our personal identity. Even if a person is born with sexual desires toward the same sex, they are still innately either a male or female and a son or daughter of God.

When someone discovers a sexual attraction toward the same sex it's important to surrender that attraction to the grace of God for self-control and healing. By analogy, it would be similar to a husband or wife who suddenly "falls in love" with a co-worker. They could argue that this attraction is so strong that they should be able to act on it because it is just natural and meant to be. Of course this is not a perfect comparison but it does get at the idea that one's sexual desires cannot be trusted and should not be the guide for life decisions.

With the above said it's important to say directly that sexual activity between those of the same sex is naturally and intrinsically disordered and, therefore, always wrong. Believing this will require that one move beyond what society holds up as acceptable as well as moving beyond what one's sexual desires are drawn to. It also is essential that we not enter into a condemning or harsh attitude. It does no good to point the finger and condemn another. Those with homosexual desires need to be treated with the utmost personal respect. Some will conclude that respect means we condone that they act on these desires. But the truth is that respect for the person means we seek to help them understand the truth of their dignity and the natural design of God in their lives. The goal must be to embrace the natural plan and design of God and choose that. If one's sexual desires are not set on the opposite sex and, thus, they choose not to enter into a male/female marriage, then celibacy and chastity must be the goal surrendering sexual activity as a sacrifice to God.

Practical Considerations

As with the other Commandments, let's look at how the Sixth Commandment rises to the level of mortal sin as well as diminishing factors that cause a sin to be venial.

Grave Matter: Serious violations against this Commandment have been identified above and include the following: Direct adultery, fornication, masturbation, pornography, polygamy, rape, contraception, prostitution, rape, free unions, homosexual sex, etc. Any direct commission of these actions is gravely wrong and contrary to the natural design of sexuality.

Full Knowledge: It is conceivable that one would lack the full knowledge of the gravity of one of these offenses for a variety of reasons. For example, say a teen is told by a parent that going on contraception is normal and should be done. The teen gets married and continues to presume that contraception is normal and nothing is wrong with it. In this case, contraception is still a grave violation against the natural order but it's possible that the couple will not be held fully guilty of grave sin because of a lack of knowledge. The same confusion could be applied to some of the other sins mentioned above. However, it's very hard to accept that sins like rape could ever be thought of as OK. That violent act should be known to be gravely disordered without ever having to be taught about it.

Complete Consent of the Will: Sexuality is an area where grave actions may not always rise to the level of mortal sin. The reason is that sexuality is a very powerful passion and has the potential of overwhelming someone to the point that they are not fully free to chose. For example, the extreme availability of pornography can create such a severe temptation for men in particular that they may find themselves clicking on images even though they know they shouldn't. It often happens that, in a moment of weakness, a man (and also women) feels he cannot resist a temptation. As always, this does not make the choice to look at pornography OK, but if he does so out of some powerful passion or past habit, he may not actually be guilty of mortal sin. It should still be confessed but it's important to understand that extreme temptation can actually have the effect of reducing one's personal guilt.

However, this understanding could be a slippery slope if a man simply says, "Well, I shouldn't look at this but I'll do it because it's just too hard to resist and God understands." Yes, God understands, but what He understands more than anything is that this is weakness that must be surrendered over to Him so that even the smallest of temptations are overcome.

Venial Sins: When any one of the above factors is not fully met the sin is venial rather than mortal. The best way to overcome all venial sins in this area is to prayerfully ponder the first part of this chapter on chastity and purity. Strive for those virtues and let them order your sexual desires in accord with the holy plan of God.

The Ninth Commandment:

You shall not covet your neighbor's wife. (Ex 20:17)

While the Sixth Commandment forbids impure actions, the Ninth Commandment takes things even further. Jesus said that, "Everyone who looks at a woman with lust has already committed adultery with her in his heart" (Matthew 5:28). The Ninth Commandment is ultimately about every form of interior impure desire and every form of covetousness.

If someone fosters a desire for impure actions with someone, the Ninth Commandment is broken even if he/she does not act on these desires. Furthermore, covetousness is a form of desire for that which is not yours. In this Commandment, one sins if he/she willfully desires someone else's spouse.

One important distinction to make here is the difference between a temptation and a willful covetous or impure desire. A temptation is something we cannot avoid and is not sinful. But temptations become sins when time and energy is given over to the temptation even in an interior way.

The key thing to understand is that we all struggle with what we call "concupiscence." Concupiscence is a term used to name the interior tendency we all have as a result of Original Sin regarding fleshly desires.

Because of our fallen human nature, we tend to look at others in a disordered and impure way. Some may have built up strong virtues that help overcome these tendencies, while others may struggle daily or even many times throughout the day.

Concupiscence is also understood as the interior tension we find between our spirit and flesh. Our spirit, when united to Christ, longs for holiness and longs to see all people in a dignified way. Our flesh, on the other hand, seriously struggles to desire what God wants us to desire. There is, therefore, an interior tension we find between our spirit and our flesh. Our flesh pushes us to act contrary to what is good and reasonable, so as to fulfill certain disordered and selfish desires. The greatest virtue we can foster to overcome these tendencies is purity of heart.

Purity

The Sixth Beatitude states, "Blessed are the clean of heart, for they will see God" (Matthew 5:8). Purity of heart means that we strive to live our sexuality in accord with the truth of God. Furthermore, it calls us to embrace all the many truths of God and all that is revealed to us by our faith. Simply put, purity is about the truth of who we are and what God calls us to. It's living in honesty and integrity in accord with our nature, our dignity and the dignity of others.

Jesus Himself said, "If you remain in my word, you will truly be my disciples, and you will know the truth, and the truth will set you free" (John 8:31-32). The Truth will set us free to love in the way God wants us to love. We will be free from fleshly desires and be free to love as we are called to love when we embrace the full truth of our sexuality. On the other hand, if we embrace the errors about our distorted and fallen human nature, we will become slaves of our flesh and slaves of concupiscence.

True purity of heart enables us to "see God" in the sense that we see clearly. The confusion and distortion of our many desires is clarified and purified. We suddenly learn to love God and, in that love of God, we also learn to love our neighbor as we ought. We love others with a pure and holy heart.

The *Catechism* (#2520) identifies the following as qualities we will discover when we become pure of heart. It states that we will prevail in purity by the following ways:

–by the *virtue* and *gift of chastity*, for chastity lets us love with upright and undivided heart;
–by *purity of intention* which consists in seeking the true end of man: with simplicity of vision, the baptized person seeks to find and to fulfill God's will in everything (Cf. Rom 12:2; Col 1:10);
–by *purity of vision*, external and internal; by discipline of feelings and imagination; by refusing all complicity in impure thoughts that incline us to turn aside from the path of God's commandments: "Appearance arouses yearning in fools" (Wis 15:5);
–by prayer:

Modesty: "Modesty protects the intimate center of the person. It means refusing to unveil what should remain hidden" (*CCC* #2521). Modesty is about being decent in every way. It acknowledges that I can be a temptation for another and, thus, avoids acting as a stumbling block for another. Modesty affects the choice of clothing and the guarding of one's eyes. It tempers unhealthy curiosity, enables one to refrain from voyeuristic explorations of an impure nature, and helps temper interests in salacious media, images and advertisements.

Social Climate: One of the most serious attacks upon purity comes from a disordered culture. Too often there are media images, advertisements, and weak social morals that bombard us constantly. Society has a duty to promote decency and purity in all its forms so as to help individuals on their mission of purity.

Purity and respect for the dignity of the person must be central in our education systems and all forms of social communication. Businesses should strive to promote chaste advertisements and entertainment. And individuals should refrain from supporting those parts of society that are contrary to the purity of heart to which we are all called.

Other Considerations

Coveting can include more than just lust and impurity. It can also move into many areas of desire. A spouse could fall into the trap of seeing good qualities in another person's spouse and desire those qualities.

Though this may not be immediately sinful, it could lead to sin when it becomes covetousness. For example, say your neighbor or co-worker seems to have an ideal marriage. You, on the other hand do not. Instead of prayerfully seeking ways to improve your marriage you spend excessive time envying the other marriage and stewing over the desire for what they have. If the other good marriage acts as an inspiration for you in your marriage, this is good. If it leads to sadness, envy and jealousy, this can be a form of covetousness.

Though this covetousness can lead to adultery and impurity, it may not. Even if it doesn't lead to adultery, which is a breaking of the Sixth Commandment, it is a sin against the Ninth Commandment.

The Bottom Line and the Upper Limit

The bottom line is that sexual temptations are real and very powerful. All of us must strive for purity of our thoughts and desires as well as in our actions. When this Beatitude is our goal, we will begin to realize that we can love on a whole new level. And we will begin to discover that we have much more energy for healthy love and wholesome living.

7

STEALING AND COVETING

The Seventh Commandment:

You shall not steal. (Ex 20:15)

The seventh commandment forbids unjustly taking or keeping the goods of one's neighbor and wronging him in any way with respect to his goods. It commands justice and charity in the care of earthly goods and the fruits of men's labor. For the sake of the common good, it requires respect for the universal destination of goods and respect for the right to private property. (*CCC* #2401)

It should be obvious to all of us that stealing is wrong. Children often struggle with thinking they have a right to what they want when they want it. For example, small children may suddenly take another child's toy because they want it. It's hard for them to understand that the toy they so deeply desire at that moment is not theirs. But as they grow, they become aware of the fact that they do not have a right to take what is not theirs. Though the concept of stealing may not be fully understood as children, it is something that most people eventually can figure out without having to be told. This reveals that the Commandment forbidding stealing is part of God's natural law and makes sense to all who have common sense and human reason.

But this Commandment takes us even further than the simple notion that stealing is wrong. It ultimately reveals to us that all of creation belongs to God and we are simply the stewards. It ultimately reveals a respect for the poor and instills a desire to care for those in need.

We begin by looking at the purpose of material goods in God's plan and move deeper from there. By understanding the big picture of the material world we will be more easily able to apply these principles to particular situations in life.

Is It Mine or Is It Yours?

Everything we have is God's. God is the giver of all good things and that even includes the gifts of the Earth. Land, property, housing, personal belongings, etc., all properly belong to God.

With that said, God has given us a share in His riches. This first and foremost applies to our life of grace and all good spiritual things. But it also applies to material wealth. God allows us to claim certain possessions as our own and calls us to respect the fact that He has given ownership of other possessions to others.

So the first thing to understand is that all we have is a gift and is ultimately from God. Furthermore, we are privileged to be able to claim some goods as our own possessions. We have a right to what we own only because of God's goodness and His choice to allow us to share in His riches. But this right to share in the riches of God is not absolute! My possession of material things must always and everywhere be seen in the light of them being a gift from God to be used for the glory of God and the good of others.

This is a hard concept to understand at times but is essential. It requires that we see the need for generosity in the same way that God is generous with us. And, at times, we should even come to realize that what God gave me was given to me so that I could share it with others. This is a very important concept to understand if we desire to continue to receive every good thing from God.

The Bottom Line

There are various ways that this Commandment is broken. Below is a summary of the most obvious and common ways:

Theft: Is theft simply the taking of something that does not belong to me against the will of the owner? No, not really. Theft must be more narrowly defined. Theft is the taking of something that does not belong to me <u>and</u> that I do not have a right to take.

For example, say you are hiking through the forest in the winter and you get lost all day. The sun is setting, it's freezing out and you fear for your life. You stumble upon a cabin in the woods and no one is there. Do you have a right to break in, stay the night, get warm and even eat some of the food in the cupboard? Is that theft? No it's not theft and yes you do have a right to do so. Of course, it would be morally upright of you to then try and replace those items when you are able.

What this example reveals is that the right to ownership of private property is not absolute. This right does not supersede the well-being and safety of your own life or the life of another. Taking what is not yours is only theft (and a sin) when doing so is unjustified and unreasonable. Prudence must be the guide for this.

Selfishness: Under the general heading of "selfishness" there are many particular sins. Here are some common ones covering a wide variety of actions:

- Failure to be generous when generosity is demanded of us by God and human reason.
- In business, manipulating the price of goods for selfish reasons. This is especially sinful when it does harm to others. This would especially apply to corporations or to anyone who has the power to do so.
- Exercising your influence or power over those in authority to make decisions to your personal benefit. This is especially sinful when those decisions are harmful to others while they benefit you.
- Misusing goods from your employer or another organization that do not belong to you.
- Wasteful use of time at work or work that is negligent or done poorly.
- Tax fraud.
- Forgery of bank accounts.
- Wasteful spending or excessive and superfluous spending, especially on yourself.
- Damaging public property intentionally and without a justified purpose.

- The willful and unjustified breaking of a legitimate contract between persons or even with a corporation or government.
- Cheating at games, especially when gambling is involved. Gambling is not sinful in itself as long as it is done with moderation and does not involve excessive risk. But excessive gambling or cheating so as to win a wager is sinful.
- Buying and selling of persons (slavery) is not only a sin against human dignity, but is also a form of theft in that persons are not possessions and should not be treated in this selfish way.

These are but a few examples of selfishness. However, there are countless ways that excessive self-focus, greed, and a desire for more can lead to sinful actions that harm ourselves and do harm to others. Selfishness is a form of stealing in that we take or refuse to give up something we do not have a right to.

Respect for Creation: God gave us dominion over all of creation. For that reason, we have a right to use the created world for our good. This includes the use of animals, plants, minerals, and other natural resources. However, this can also be abused.

Natural Resources: The resources of the Earth are meant for the common good of all people. Therefore, if individuals, corporations, or even governments abuse the use of resources for selfish reasons they are stealing from the common good. There are numerous ways that abuse of the resources of the Earth can take place. For example, the complete destruction of a rainforest for the purpose of certain individuals getting rich would be a form of stealing from nature and a sin against the common good for selfish reasons. It would include any unreasonable and excessive use of natural goods that is destructive to this or future generations.

Animals: Animals are part of God's creation and must be respected. The intentional and irrational abuse of animals for the purpose of selfish pleasure is evil and a form of stealing in that it is an abuse of our "dominion" over creation. However, it is within the reasonable limits of dominion over animals to use them for food, clothing or domestic chores. It is also permitted to hunt animals for sport as long as this is done in humane ways. Ideally, the animal will also then be used for food or clothing. Sometimes it is also legitimate to eradicate animals for the common good or for their own good and survival as a species. For example, if a certain breed of animal is overpopulated it may be in the best interest of that species or in the best interest of the common good that the legitimate authority call for additional hunting or thinning of the herd.

It is proper to care for animals that are domesticated such as by bringing them to a veterinarian. However, the good health of an animal must not become excessive. It would be wrong to spend excessive amounts of money on the health of an animal when that money could be spent on other needs of the common good which are of greater importance. In other words, the good health of a domesticated animal is not the same as the good health of a human. Furthermore, the euthanasia of ill or old animals is legitimate and, at times, required out of respect for the animal and the common good.

The Dignity of the Human Person and the Economy

The Sixth Commandment applies not only to individuals, but also to various economic systems and systems of governance. There is a rich tradition in our Church of what we call the "Social Doctrine" or "Social Teaching." Politics and economics are very important parts of human life and the many systems of governance and modern economics raise important moral questions. The development of our economic teachings is especially the fruit of the nineteenth century with the advent of technology, industry, mass production, new labor practices, etc. The Church provides some basic guidelines and moral principles to follow. These teachings fall under the Seventh Commandment in so far as they have to do with the use of resources, the exchange of money and human labor. Below are some of those teachings:

Dignity of Work: God gave humanity dominion over the created world (Genesis 1:28). However, as a result of Original Sin, the man was given the punishment of having to provide for himself and his family by the sweat of his brow (Genesis 3:17-19). Though this is an unfortunate result of Original Sin, it also becomes a source of redemption and dignity. "Work" becomes a means of exercising dominion over creation and enables man to cooperate with God in His divine work of Creation. For this reason, work has dignity and humanity discovers a certain dignity in proper work. Through work, we are able to care for and provide for ourselves and our families. This is not only a basic human right but also a basic human duty. In fact, if one were to ignore work and fail to be productive in some way, this would be a violation of their basic dignity as a person and a violation of one's basic duty in life.

All economic systems, work-related laws and private business practices must have as the primary focus the dignity of the person and their right to work so as to share in the dignity of God's creative activity. This is a hard sell for many modern business leaders but must always be the central guiding principle for all work-related activity and decisions. Profit must not be the ultimate driving force; rather, the dignity of the person and the dignity of work must be the driving force.

Profit vs. Person: "Any system in which social relationships are determined entirely by economic factors is contrary to the nature of the human person and his acts" (*CCC* #2423). This is a key principle that should be considered with any economic system. If "profit" is the primary goal of an economic system, it is a problematic system. Yes, this is a hard "pill" to swallow in our modern age and in many modern forms of businesses. The reason for this is that when profit is the ultimate goal and end, the dignity of the person will inevitably take the back seat. This is immoral. Profit must obviously be considered as a goal since profit in a business is good for people working there. But when decisions are made purely based on furthering profit, this leads to the lessening of the dignity of the individual and must be avoided even if it means less profit. Practically speaking, those in authority have to make the best decision they can, keeping centrally in mind the dignity of the worker. It is understood that good minds may disagree about what is best, overall, for the health of the business and, therefore, what is best for those who work there. The duty of the Church is to simply keep the dignity of the person front and center so that the best practical decisions are made for the betterment of all. It is also understandable that, at times, layoffs or reduction in pay may be what is best for the dignity of the people involved. Though this may be painful at times to accept and decide upon, it is left up to the good prudential judgment of those in charge as long as they keep the general principles laid out here as the guiding factor of their decisions.

Production vs. Person: Basic human rights, both of the individual and groupings of people, must always be more important in making economic decisions than production. People are not just a means to the end of making a product or making money. The person must always be considered first. Excessive burdens imposed on the worker so as to increase production should be avoided. This is especially true when productivity at work affects the person's family and spiritual life. For example, requiring excessive hours to the detriment of the personal and family life of employees is immoral.

Capitalism vs. Person: But what about modern Capitalism? Though there are many dangers within that system, it can be a system that respects the rights and dignity of the person while, at the same time, is quite productive. Much could be said about this but, for our purposes here, suffice it to say that as long as the dignity of the person, the employee, the consumer, etc. is of central focus, this system can be good and morally upright.

Capitalism has been suggested to have one particular moral virtue that should be identified here. Some have suggested that capitalism, with its basic "supply and demand" philosophy, has the potential to bring forth human ingenuity and creativity. When a capitalistic system has as its goal the good of the consumer, creativity will be used to meet those needs and produce a profit. This can be very good and healthy. In this case, excessive governmental regulations could help to temper greed, but could also hinder creativity. Balance must be the goal so that human dignity is always respected and personal creativity is fostered.

Fair Wage: "A worker deserves his pay" (1 Timothy 5:18). It can be a strong temptation for those who are business owners to pay an unjust wage if they can get away with it. It can be reasoned that, if people are willing to work for a low wage, we can pay that wage. But this is a slippery slope and could lead to immoral practices. Remember, the key focus must be the worker not the profit. Sure, profit is important so that the business can grow and more people can be employed. But human prudence must enter in and temperance must be exercised in making decisions regarding the amount of pay.

The bottom line is that a worker must be paid a sufficient amount to care for himself and his family. Care should also be taken that those in authority do not become excessively rich to the detriment of others. Obtaining wealth is not immoral but it can lead to many temptations.

Therefore, those in authority within businesses must consider everyone when setting a proper wage.

Reaching Out to the Poor

Jesus said that we will always have the poor with us (John 12:8). Poverty is a result of the fallen human condition we find ourselves in. There are many forms of poverty. There are those who are spiritually poor, lacking the Gospel and grace. There are those who suffer illness and other tragedies through no fault of their own. There are those who are born into poverty and, despite their best efforts, cannot escape it. There are those who barely make it day-to-day but do have enough to survive. And, of course, there are those who out of personal neglect and irresponsible living find themselves in dire need.

Assisting those in dire need is an essential duty of the Gospel. Regardless of why someone is in dire need, we must help them when we find them in this state. Therefore, on a local level especially, it is necessary that we make sure all people have their basic human needs met. Food, shelter, clothing, etc., is a requirement of human dignity.

Some argue that caring for the poor is a way of enabling them to continue to live irresponsibly. Perhaps this is true in some contexts. But this is more their concern than ours. Our duty is to reach out to those in need regardless of why they are in the state of need. We ought not discriminate when we find someone in need. Mercy means we love because a person is worthy of love and not because they have shown that they deserve it. They deserve it simply because they are human.

With that said, it is in accord with human reason that we expect the poor to begin to take on responsibility for themselves and their families. Therefore, tying assistance for the needy to systems which also foster personal responsibility is quite appropriate. There will always be times when direct and immediate assistance is necessary and proper. But there are also reasonable ways to offer assistance with the expectation of personal responsibility. This, too, is an act of love.

The mission of the Church is not to define any one particular economic or political system so as to care for the needs of the poor. Intelligent minds may disagree on the best approach. It is the mission of the

Church to simply keep the poor before the eyes of all, especially those in authority and with wealth, so that they can prudently fulfill their duty to help those in need in the proper way.

In the modern world, addressing poverty globally is a new concern. In the past, global poverty was not as well known by all and wealthy nations were not always in the practical position of offering mass relief and assistance when needed. Caring for the poor was something done at home and within the local community.

Today, those with wealth are in a position to reach out to those in poverty in new and productive ways. For example, international humanitarian organizations make it easier to do this across national borders. Helping the poor, in these cases, is not so much just a matter of taking care of their temporary needs. Rather, it's a matter of assisting poorer countries with the proper education and means necessary to help them care for themselves and eradicate poverty. Let's reflect upon the duty of nations with regard to this Commandment.

International Considerations

Human communities are defined on various levels. The most basic level is that of the family. From there we can see the human family expanding to local communities, states, nations and, ultimately, the world. Typically, each community holds something in common that unites them. Language, culture, common experience, common commitment, laws, etc. are among those things which help bring unity and solidarity among peoples.

Especially today, in our global world of communication, we must strive to offer respect, support and concern for those of other nations and cultures. Though we may have various differences, we must hold in common a basic respect and concern for every person and every grouping of persons.

Most importantly, as Christians, we have a duty to spread the Gospel globally. We must do so with our words, but also with our actions. We must seek peace among nations, but peace is achieved especially through the Gospel and all that the Gospel calls us to.

This Commandment particularly calls us to a respect for the material resources of other nations. We are called to seek the good and healthy economic development of nations, especially those nations that are poor and in dire need of development. It is a moral obligation of the wealthy and productive nations to have concern for those nations that live in poverty or economic, political and social chaos. There are many factors that contribute to the hardships of some nations. It is not proper for the wealthy and productive nations to sit on the sidelines and watch others suffer. Rather, various forms of direct aid must be given out of respect for the dignity of all.

At times, direct and immediate aid is necessary. This duty flows from our calling of charity. When tragedy, poverty, famine, or the like strike a foreign nation, those nations who are able to help do have a moral duty to do so.

Aid must go beyond the immediate relief of those in dire consequences. Working with other nations to help them develop healthy economies so as to become productive and self-sustaining is essential.

Education is one of the most important ways that developed nations can assist with those in need. Additionally, making sure that poor countries are not taken advantage of is a matter of basic respect for the dignity of all. By sincerely caring for those in need, educating them, assisting with fair economic trade and the like will help ensure that everyone, and every nation, will have the ability to fulfill the dignity of work.

The responsibility of assisting nations is not first and foremost that of the pastors of the Church. Pastors must preach the Gospel and reach out to the poor and those in need. But the primary responsibility for economic development and the transformation of a society regarding work and productivity is that of the laity: laity as individuals, but also laity within the political structures. Those in authority must especially see it as their duty to help foster world-wide communion and assistance to the needy.

World peace is obtainable and must be our constant goal. And the material, educational, and economic support we owe each nation should never be underestimated as a necessary means to achieve this important goal.

The Tenth Commandment:

> You shall not covet your neighbor's house. You shall not covet your neighbor's wife, his male or female slave, his ox or donkey, or anything that belongs to your neighbor. (Ex 20:17)

> For where your treasure is, there also will your heart be. (Mt 6:21)

> The tenth commandment unfolds and completes the ninth, which is concerned with concupiscence of the flesh. It forbids coveting the goods of another, as the root of theft, robbery, and fraud, which the seventh commandment forbids...The tenth commandment concerns the intentions of the heart; with the ninth, it summarizes all the precepts of the Law. (*CCC* #2534)

In addition to completing the Ninth Commandment on coveting, the Tenth Commandment also completes the Seventh Commandment regarding stealing. The Seventh Commandment especially focuses upon the <u>exterior actions</u> regarding stealing, poverty, social justice, etc. The Tenth Commandment goes beyond the exterior actions by seeking to purify even the intentions of the heart. It is fair to say that those sins forbidden by the Tenth Commandment are the roots of those sins forbidden by the Seventh Commandment. In other words, the interior coveting of material wealth (Tenth Commandment), leads to stealing and selfishness in various forms (Seventh Commandment).

The Root of the Problem: He Who Has Money Never Has Money Enough

When you are hungry, you desire food. When you are tired, you desire sleep. These are natural reactions to those things we lack and need. We need food and sleep. Therefore, we should naturally desire them.

The problem is that our desires can easily get out of control and far exceed that which is reasonable and proper. Sometimes we get angry and desire revenge. Or get our paycheck and desire much more. If we let our desires control us we can be certain that we would never be satisfied. Disordered desires will never be satisfied with an abundance of food, alcohol, sex, money, revenge, etc.

This Commandment especially focuses in on one desire that is easily distorted - the desire for material wealth. As one ancient Roman Catechism states, "He who has money never has money enough." What a profound truth to understand. It simply means that a distorted desire for money is never actually satisfied with the obtainment of money. It only leads to a stronger desire for more.

Think about it. If someone longs for money will they be satisfied once they gain a million dollars? When they achieve the goal of being a millionaire will they then sit back and say, "Now my life is complete! I'm a millionaire and I do not desire anything more!" Will they be fully satisfied with that million dollars? Or will they immediately start thinking about how they can turn that million into two, three, five or more? If they are irrationally attached to the million they just obtained you can be certain that they will not be satisfied with it. They will be tempted to want more, and more and then some more.

So what's the problem you say? The problem is that if we constantly long for more and more money we are fooling ourselves into thinking that more and more will satisfy us. It's foolishness to think this and we are being foolish if we fall into this trap. We need to get to the heart of the problem and deal with it in its roots.

So what's the root of the problem? The root of the problem is a disordered and extreme desire for "stuff." This disordered desire grows when it is fed with more of *this or that*, or when it sees *this or that* and cannot obtain it. This desire is based on irrationality in that there is an irrational and erroneous conviction that *this or that* will satisfy the disordered desire. The problem is that even if the disordered desire is fulfilled, it will quickly lose that instant satisfaction left only desiring more.

These disordered desires affect people in many practical ways. Sometimes a desire for more will lead one to desire the misfortune of others or, at very least, lead one to take delight in the misfortune of others if the effect of that misfortune is their own financial gain. Here are a few examples of this kind of disordered desire:

- A farmer of corn who hopes every other farmer's corn crop goes bad so that his corn will be able to be sold for more.
- A physician who gets excited because of a serious disease. This

disease means more patients and more money.

- A lawyer who gets excited at potential lawsuits because it means more money.

The real question is this: Do you desire to make a profit from the misfortune of others? If so, it reveals that your desires are truly disordered.

Envy is another danger in our disordered desires and is a fruit of this covetousness forbidden by the Tenth Commandment. Envy is a form of sorrow at the success of others. Coveting is more of the wanting of another's goods, and envy adds to it discontentment, ill will, sorrow or even resentment toward another whom you covet. So, for example, if someone close to you enters into a legitimate business endeavor and has great success, how does that make you feel? Are you excited for them? Or do you discover a certain sorrow over their success wishing that their success was yours? If you see that desire, then you can be certain that it's the ugly sin of envy.

Getting in Order!

Blessed are the poor in spirit, for theirs is the Kingdom of Heaven (Matthew 5:3).

Blessed are the clean of heart, for they will see God (Matthew 5:8).

Striving for and obtaining the Beatitudes bring about fulfillment of the Christian life. It's what we are made for. The Beatitudes reveal the deepest truth of who we are and what life is all about.

The Tenth Commandment especially calls us to poverty and purity of heart. The reward of these blessings is total fulfillment in God's Kingdom. They enable us to see God!

All of the Beatitudes enable us to abandon ourselves to the providence of God and embrace His law of charity. First, we love God with our whole being, and from that love, we live a life of charity toward others.

The Beatitudes not only enable us to make the right choices, they also purify our desires. This is so very important to understand! When we begin to enter into the heights of perfection, we will begin to discover that even our desires are re-ordered by God. We will want to see God. We will long for God and desire Him above all else. And in this growing desire for God, we will begin to realize that our disordered desires start to fade away. We will no longer desire earthly wealth in an irrational and distorted way. Instead, all the desires of the Earth and the flesh will be put in perspective and purified. In their place, the overriding longing of our hearts will be for God and holiness of life. And this longing will become fulfilled in an ever-deepening way as we are freed of the many unhealthy attachments we have.

It's important to realize that our desires are good and were created by God. And when they are properly ordered, we reap abundant satisfaction and fulfillment in life through them. When they are disordered, they enslave us and lure us into countless empty promises of happiness. The choice is ours.

8

THE TRUTH WILL SET YOU FREE!

The Eighth Commandment:

You shall not bear false witness against your neighbor. (Ex 20:16)

Again you have heard that it was said to your ancestors, "Do not take a false oath, but make good to the Lord all that you vow." But I say to you, do not swear at all... (Mt 5:33)

The eighth commandment forbids misrepresenting the truth in our relations with others. (*CCC* #2464)

Jesus is "the way and the truth and the life..." (John 14:6) and is "full of grace and truth" (John 1:14). What does this mean? First, it means that He Himself is the full revelation of all that is true. He is truth itself and His life, death and resurrection reveals the deepest truths of humanity. Jesus Himself reveal to us what life is all about, what salvation is and who God is. He is the full revelation of the Father (John 12:45). Knowing Him is knowing Truth itself.

So what does that all mean, you ask? How is Jesus the truth and the full revelation of the Father? At the risk of sounding like that is an unanswerable question, suffice it to say that this "mystery" is the entire goal of this chapter and this Commandment. Understanding Truth is our goal. This Commandment is not only about telling the truth and avoiding lies, it is even more so about seeking Him who is Truth itself and entering into the Truth in every way.

As Christians, we are called to live in the truth. This means that as Christ Jesus lives in us and we in Him, we must speak and act in accord with all that is true. Discovering and living the truth are what fulfills our dignity as persons.

The Eighth Commandment calls us to be people of the Truth. We are to live lives of honesty and sincerity. Living a genuine life of integrity and truthfulness is essential to who we are. This Commandment calls us not only to avoid falsity, it also calls us to enter daily into the deepest and most profound truths of life, seeking to know and live these truths in their fullness.

As we come to know and live the truth, we are called to bear witness to that truth; we are called to bear witness to our faith and to Christ Himself. This is done in many ways through our words and our actions. The witness of charity is a powerful sign of our commitment to the full truth of the Gospel.

One of the greatest forms of love is martyrdom. Martyrdom is a public witness of the love of God. It's the ultimate statement that one loves God even more than life itself and is committed to the fullness of Truth even if this witness requires the ultimate sacrifice. Throughout history, the Church has held up many martyrs for all to see. The blood of martyrs has become the seed of faith for many because of their ultimate witness to the truth.

The Bottom Line: Offenses Against the Truth

There are many ways in which this Commandment is directly violated. Below are some of the most obvious ways identified by the *Catechism*.

Lying: Lying is pretty straight forward, or is it? Blatant lies may be straight forward but there are forms of lies that are not as clear cut and not as obvious. Lying can be done in various ways. First, a lie is committed when someone intentionally and willfully falsifies the facts to one or more persons. This intentional and willful deceit is grave when that which is lied about is of a more serious nature. Any direct and intentional misrepresentation of the facts is grave matter.

However, sometimes we speak of "white lies" to identify those lies that are less serious but still lies. For example, if someone asked you if you like the meal they just cooked and you say it is "very good" even though it is not, this may be considered a "white lie." Care must be taken to avoid even white lies. However, with that said, we are not automatically obliged to speak hurtful truths to others.

Lies can also be committed through the omission of facts. We call this a "lie by omission." Omitting certain facts can, at times, be even more damaging than an outright falsification of facts because of the malicious and deceitful nature of this form of lie. For example, say a car salesman is trying to sell a used car and tells the potential buyer that the odometer has 75,000 miles on it. But he then fails to say that the odometer was actually taken from another car and put in this one because the car being sold actually has 150,000 miles on it. What he said is true: "the odometer has 75,000 miles on it." But it is clearly a deception by failing to reveal that the current odometer is not the original odometer to the car.

Perjury: Perjury is a lie told under oath, typically in a civil court. Perjury is especially serious when the lie does damage to another. For example, if lying in a trial leads to the false conviction of a person, then the perjury is very grave. As mentioned above, a lie can also be an act of omission of facts. Therefore, if someone knowingly withholds facts in a civil proceeding or under oath, they sin. Even if they do not technically break the civil law of perjury by withholding essential facts, they still sin before God for their failure to reveal the whole truth.

The Good Name of Others: The Church has always seen the importance of a good reputation and the gravity of harming another's good name. Harm can be done to another's good name in many ways. Direct and malicious lies as well as the willful withholding of important facts that should be said are all included as sins against the Eighth Commandment. It is also sinful to reveal "truths" that should not be revealed.

The *Catechism* (#2477) gives a very clear explanation of these offenses against a person's good reputation which is worth quoting in its entirety:

Respect for the reputation of persons forbids every attitude and word likely to cause them unjust injury (Cf. CIC, can. 220). He becomes guilty:
  –of *rash judgment* who, even tacitly, assumes as true, without sufficient foundation, the moral fault of a neighbor;
  –of *detraction* who, without objectively valid reason, discloses another's faults and failings to persons who did not know them; (Cf. Sir 21:28)

—of *calumny* who, by remarks contrary to the truth, harms the reputation of others and gives occasion for false judgments concerning them.

Notice that there are three levels of sins against the truth identified. First, there are rash judgments. This tells us we ought not presume the worst. Rash judgment is something that may never be spoken but simply thought of interiorly. Even this does damage to another and is contrary to the truth.

Second, detraction is identified. This is speaking of something that is true to those who do not have a right to hear it. Gossip, for example, is a form of detraction. Even though what is said is true, it is still a sin against the Eighth Commandment since it is a truth that should not have been revealed to another.

Third, calumny is speaking something that is false and defamatory to another. This is the worst sin against the good reputation of another. When the good name of another is harmed in one of the ways mentioned above, reparation must be made. First, interior repentance must be made but that is not enough. As far as possible, the sinner must do all that is reasonable and charitable to restore the good name of the person they hurt.

Boasting: Boasting, or bragging, may not at first be thought of as a sin; but it is. Similar to calumny and detraction, boasting is the revealing of things that are true about you in either a disordered way or in a prideful and self-gratifying way. It's the act of attention seeking and is contrary to the deepest truths of humility. Similarly, flattery of another is deceitful and a sin against this Commandment.

Do I Have A Right to Know?

In our day and age, we tend to think we have a right to know just about everything about everyone. Social media, especially, has opened up the daily lives of many people in such a way that personal privacy is often seen as unimportant. Below are some guidelines regarding the dissemination of information and the right to privacy.

Right to Privacy: The right to privacy simply means that not everyone has a right to know everything about us and our private lives. Even those who are public persons, such as politicians, deserve to have their private lives kept private.

One of the most obvious examples of this is the Sacrament of Confession. The seal of the confessional is absolute. This means that there are no conditions in which a confessor may reveal the content of a person's confession. This is not just a sacramental law of the Church; it also reveals the God-given right to privacy. There are many things that only God has a right to know. There are other things that close family and friends should be made aware of in our lives. And there are only certain parts of our private lives that everyone should have a right to know.

When details of our private life must be known for the common good, it is permissible that these facts be shared. For example, if someone commits a murder in private, this action must be made public for the common good.

Professional secrets: There are many situations, of a professional nature, in which people have a duty to keep confidentiality. In these cases, the truth is not for public dissemination. For example, a medical doctor must keep medical records confidential. Or those in government may need to keep certain internal facts confidential so as to protect the good reputation of others or to protect the common good. As with many other examples, not everyone has a right to know everything about everyone or every situation. Keeping confidentiality in these cases is a requirement of the Eighth Commandment.

Media: The media is to serve the common good by the dissemination of the truth. They have an obligation to share with the public those things that serve the interests and good of all. However, their right to share the truth in a public way must be exercised in such a way that the rights of the individual and the inherent right to privacy are not abused.

Furthermore, the media has a duty to disseminate the entire truth, not just partial truths. One erroneous form of reporting is called "exclusionary detailing." This is the commission of a "lie by omission" of certain facts, or the negligent failure to correct a misconception. When the media fails to present the full truth, or correct a misconception, then those within the media are guilty of breaking the Eighth Commandment.

The Upper Limit: Art, Beauty and the Pursuit of Truth

A final consideration has to do with the pursuit of the truth. The Eighth Commandment is not only about refraining from a lie; it is also about seeking Truth itself.

The Truth, with a capital "T" is ultimately defined as a person, a divine Person. And that Person is Jesus Christ and all that He has revealed to us. Seeking the Truth means we seek Jesus Himself. First and foremost, this is fulfilled by choosing to enter into the Gospel and to seek the many truths of our faith. We break this Commandment when we are lazy in the deepening of our faith. We fulfill this Commandment when we seek the many truths of our faith and enter into them wholeheartedly.

Truth is also revealed in beauty. And beauty is discovered in many ways. Beauty is discovered in nature, in each person, in music, in sacred art, etc. Therefore, this Commandment calls us to seek true objective beauty.

Sacred art, for example, is a reflection of true beauty and, therefore, we have a duty to foster sacred art insofar as it is a reflection of true beauty. The arts, therefore, should be held up as an important part of society and the healthy development of culture and human life. But the arts can also be used for ill. Art, in and of itself, is a neutral means of expressing oneself as well as a means of expressing objective realities. For example, art can express the disorder of chaos and confusion, or it can express the order of Heaven or the beauty of nature. As Christians, we have a duty to use art for the glory of God and the refreshment of the human spirit.

Practical Considerations

Once again, let's look at the ways that the Eighth Commandment is broken in a mortal way so that we can also see the venial ways that this Commandment is broken.

Grave Matter: Any direct dissemination of false information could be considered grave when it brings with it grave consequences. This may be hard to define in certain terms so it is ultimately left up to the particular circumstances.

Let's offer one extreme example to which we will also apply the other two factors of mortal sin. Say a person is at work and comes across the fraudulent activity of another. Say that the fraudulent activity is that another employee has stolen money from the employer. The person who discovers the activity is then asked by the employer if he has come across any discrepancies. Since the employee who did the stealing is a friend, the person lies and says that the books look good.

This act of covering up the theft is a lie and is sinful. The person who discovered the stealing did have a duty to report it and the cover up was a violation of the Eighth Commandment. In fact, it is fair to say that the lie committed in the cover up is grave matter.

Full Knowledge: If the person above who discovers the stealing knows with certainty that his friend stole the money, he is most likely guilty of also having full knowledge that a cover up is a lie. What sort of diminishing factors, if any, could actually have the effect of diminishing one's personal guilt in the cover up? Two things come to mind: First, if the person is not fully convinced that the stealing took place, he may not be fully guilty of a cover up and, therefore, may not be fully guilty of lying if he fails to reveal what he knows. Second, if for some reason the person concludes that the stealing was "not that big of a deal," he may not fully <u>know</u> that he has a duty to report it. Say, for example, the "stealing" is an act that everyone does and everyone knows that everyone does it. It is possible that this could confuse the person enough to conclude that this was not a big deal and he does not have to report it.

In this case, as with all the Commandments, the confusion on the part of the person concealing the truth is not justified; but the confusion may be enough to lessen the personal responsibility to the point that it is no longer mortal sin, only venial sin. It doesn't make it right to conceal the truth, or to lie, it only makes the personal actions less serious.

Complete Consent of the Will: Continuing with the example above, say that the employee finds his friend is stealing and confronts him. He offers a tearful sob story as to why he stole money and is very sorry. He begs the friend not to tell for the sake of his wife and children. As a result, his friend does twist the facts and lies to keep his friend from getting in trouble.

This is not justified but the emotional situation and fear for his friend's future may have the effect of lessening the moral responsibility of the lie he told. He should do the right thing and must avoid telling a lie, but the situation may be such that it is only a venial sin rather than mortal.

Venial Sin: The example above, as with the examples in previous chapters, reveals the complexity of sin and moral guilt. God sees all things and calls us to holiness of life even when it is difficult. With that said, God also sees the many factors that contribute to our errors in judgment and will judge accordingly.

Conclusion

Hopefully these reflections in the preceding chapters have helped to paint a picture of the moral life. Morality is something that has been revealed by God and must be sought on a daily basis. Sin can come at any moment. Therefore, we must always strive to build up virtue so as to build up proper defenses against sin and establish habits of seeking holiness of life.

Reread any chapter that stood out to you. Reflect upon it, pray over it and ask for God's grace to live a good moral life. Morality is one of the three basic keys to holiness and happiness. The first key is faith (as explained in the first book of this series), the second key is worship (as explained in the second book of this series) and the third key is morality. Good moral living is the fruit of one's life of faith and worship. Let your faith and worship transform you into a holy and morally upright person and you will be eternally grateful for the good fruits this bears in your life and in the lives of those whom you are called to love and serve.

SMALL GROUP STUDY

One of the best ways to learn our glorious Catholic faith is through faith-based small group discussion and study. Talking about our faith brings clarity. Hearing what others have to say brings insight.

Each of the three books of the *My Catholic Life! Series* can be used as an 8 week program of Catholic study for you to engage in. This small group study program is great for these and other settings:

- **Family** – Why not gather family members together for an eight week study of our faith?!
- **Friends** – Initiate a study among your friends and invite some new friends!
- **Neighborhood** – This is a great way to evangelize right in your neighborhood. Send a letter out inviting neighbors. You just may be surprised at how many are interested!
- **Parish** – Talk to your parish priest to gain permission to begin one or more study groups at your local church.
- **R.C.I.A.** – This is a great tool to use for those becoming Catholic. All three series, together, will cover the entire *Catechism*!

Who can start a program? – This program is designed to be easy for any Catholic to organize and lead. You do not have to be an expert in the Catholic faith to take the initiative. If you feel called to take this initiative then "Be not afraid" and jump in!

What do you need? – The materials include one of the three catechetical books from the *My Catholic Life! Series* as well as the study companion which is available for free online at www.myCatholic.Life/small-group-study. So visit that link, pray, and ask our Lord how He wants you to help spread the faith!

www.myCatholic.Life

Also, download the "Catholic Daily Reflections" app for smart phones and tablets. Available through website or all app stores.

53209484R00088

Made in the USA
Lexington, KY
26 September 2019